RADICAL CHRISTIANITY
AND THE FLESH OF JESUS

Radical Christianity *and the* Flesh of Jesus

The Roots of Eucharistic Living

ARTHUR A. VOGEL

WILLIAM B. EERDMANS PUBLISHING COMPANY
GRAND RAPIDS, MICHIGAN / CAMBRIDGE, U.K.

© 1995 Wm. B. Eerdmans Publishing Co.

255 Jefferson Ave. S.E., Grand Rapids, Michigan 49503 /

P. O. Box 163, Cambridge CB3 9PU U.K.

Printed in the United States of America

00 99 98 97 96 95   7 6 5 4 3 2 1

Library of Congress Cataloging-in-Publication Data

Vogel, Arthur Anton.
Radical Christianity and the flesh of Jesus /
Arthur A. Vogel.
p.   cm.
ISBN 0-8028-0881-6 (pbk.: alk. paper)
1. Jesus Christ — Person and offices. 2. Flesh (Theology) 3. Christian life.
4. Grace (Theology) I. Title.
BT202.V593   1995
232 — dc20   95-38860
CIP

With the occasional exception, the Scripture quotations in this publication are from
the New Revised Standard Version Bible, copyright © 1989 by the Division of Christian
Education of the National Council of Churches of Christ in the U.S.A., and used by
permission.

Contents

Preface

IN OUR electronic age, with its surfeit of access to information, interactional entertainment, and the choice of hundreds — if not thousands — of programmed options to fill our time, getting people's attention in the face of constant competition has become a major goal. In the scramble to attract readers, viewers, or listeners, many claims and adjectives are incessantly overworked. "Radical" is one of the adjectives calculated to attract attention, for it promises challenge and newness, something different from the humdrum and ordinary.

"Radical," taken from the Latin word *radix,* meaning "root," is not used in the title of this book simply as an attention getter, however; it is used because it is the most appropriate word to describe a basic contention of these pages, namely, that Christianity — as our life — is rooted in the flesh. Our fleshly lives are also the key to eucharistic living, for, in the eucharist, Jesus' fleshly life enters our fleshly lives. To help us understand how that can happen and the significance of its happening is the purpose of this inquiry into eucharistic living.

ARTHUR A. VOGEL

1

The Immediacy of Our Lives

WE ALL CENTER the world of our personal experience and, by the choices we make and the activities we pursue throughout our lives, at least partially create a world within which to live. We create our worlds by our styles of living. Because those worlds are *ours,* we are comfortable in them. We are generally able to let into our worlds no more than we can handle. We make our coffee to our taste, flavor our food to suit us, play our favorite music, express our opinions about life, and associate only with people we like.

The shame of it is that the personal worlds we make never last. They all exist within a wider world we did not make, and that world, in the end, overwhelms our worlds. There is a world that receives us as well as the personal worlds we make. When we are born, that is the world we enter, and when we die, that is the world we leave. In the end, as in the beginning, *the* world is more than we are. We all go down into the dust from which we came.

For Christians, the uniqueness of Jesus of Nazareth is that somehow he was a man who was born into the world and who died in the world and yet was not defeated by the world. It is claimed that he, in some mysterious way, defeated the world by his death — normally the victory of the world — and by his life and death and living after death revealed that the world was not his source but that the source of the world is found in him. The very creation of the world is claimed somehow to have taken place through him, and the source and purpose of the world are said to be known in him.

The Gospel of John begins by stating that the Word which was with God and which was God, the Word through whom all things came into being, became flesh and lived among us in Jesus (1:1-14). The Letter to the Hebrews refers to Jesus as the Son of God, "whom he [God] appointed heir of all things, [and] through whom he also created the worlds" (1:1-2). The Letter to the Colossians speaks of our having been rescued from the old world of darkness and being brought into the reign of Jesus, God's beloved Son. Jesus is said to be "the image of the invisible God"; it is further maintained that "all things have been created through him and for him." Risen from the dead, Jesus has the "first place in everything"; "in him all things hold together," and through him God reconciled all things to himself (Col. 1:1-20).

All of the passages I have quoted are challenging in both their origin and their meaning, but they all testify to the earliest Christian experience that, in Jesus, God's ultimate presence, purpose, and supremacy are realized in his creation.

During his life on earth, Jesus centered and created a personal world, just as we do, but Christian faith asserts that, in his case, the human world was uniquely made by the One who made the world within which our personalized worlds are found — and which evolved billions of years before human beings appeared within it.

In the normal course of events, the all-inclusive world in which we live always overcomes us: we are interrupted by something we did not anticipate; we become ill; we grow old and die.

Our best plans fail, and our hopes are dashed by events in the world over which we have no control. The world remains itself, but we are unable to be ourselves in it. The worlds of our ambitions and expectations are overruled by a more inclusive world beyond them.

The hope Christians have in Jesus arises from the belief that the source of the human world he centered is the Source of the all-inclusive world that destroys our personal worlds. His personal world cannot be defeated by arbitrary or even malicious interruptions from beyond it. That makes his world a new creation springing up within the world rather than being, like ours, no more than a subsystem within the old that is finally absorbed back into the old.

Jesus comes into our world, but he comes to change it into his world. When one lives in his world, everything is different; indeed, life in Jesus' world is so different that those who have experienced it, beginning with Paul, describe it as nothing less than a new creation. To be with Jesus — to live in his presence — is to live in a new network of relations in which he is supreme. In the world he centers, Jesus is "Lord of all," as Peter proclaimed to Cornelius and his friends in Caesarea (Acts 10:36). As Lord of all, Jesus rules all.

The world in its totality is always more than we can manage, for the world is a network of conditions and events existing before us and extending beyond us, within which we live. The complexity of the world repeatedly shows itself to be too much for us totally to anticipate, to master, or to control. In our lives in the world, we are constantly engaged by and vulnerable to the world's intruding itself upon us; the fear and anxiety we know in our lives arise from the threat to our reality that the reality of the world poses for us. Because the world extends beyond us, our cares and anxieties extend beyond us in it.

On the other hand, when we know Jesus as the source of the

world in which we live, everything is changed, for, because he is the source of that world, his presence in the world extends beyond us in place and time just as the physical world does. Knowing Jesus as the source of a new network of relations constituting a new world order is our assurance that his love is able to encompass and redeem our lives no matter where we may be and no matter what may happen to us. Then the assurance of his presence coexists with the world from which our fears formerly arose; the assurance of his presence becomes the horizon of the world around us. Both his presence and the world are more than we can control, but when we live in his presence we know that unforeseen events in the world have no ultimate power over us.

Let us take a moment to go into all this more thoroughly in the act of Christian faith. At the tomb of Lazarus, Martha recognized Jesus to be "the one coming into the world" (John 11:27). The Christian life, as I have indicated, consists in our living in a new world made available to us by Jesus' coming into our world.

We may continue to consider a working definition of the world to be "the all-encompassing network of relations within which we live." *The* world is a network of relations encompassing innumerable subsystems within it — among them the worlds we make. The smaller worlds for which we are responsible often exclude each other, but nothing is excluded from *the* world. The vulnerability we know in *the* world, in contrast to the security we feel in our smaller and limited worlds, arises from the fact that in *the* world one more thing always happens! That world is beyond our control.

For Christians, the supremacy of Jesus' life, established by his resurrection from the dead, centers a new way in which our lives are interrelated with each other and with all reality. The network of relations springing from the incarnate love of God in Jesus' life extends beyond us and contains us precisely as the world itself does. Christians believe that in Jesus, the one sent into the world by God to reveal God's eternal purpose for the world (Eph. 3:11), we know and experience the final victory of God's loving will in the world. In the experience of Jesus' presence, we can relax in an "abandonment to divine providence," as the title of Jean-Pierre de Caussade's well-known book puts it. The relaxation accompanying such abandonment does not mean that we resign from the world and leave everything to God; rather, it describes our ability to abandon the burden of fear and despair as we actively live with hope in the world.

In the lordship of Jesus over evil and death, we live in a re-created world in its creative source, and, living in Jesus' presence, we experience the final victory he has already won — even though that victory has not yet been fully embodied throughout the world. In Jesus, as it has been said, we live in the beginning of salvation time, a new time signaling a new day.

In the presence of Jesus, we are given a totally new way of living. Everything in our lives is different. Even in what could be called our old location (for we do not leave the world), we find ourselves in a new situation; something new has been added that gives every event a new meaning. In the presence of Jesus, what was formerly a tomb of death is transformed into a place of life not only for Lazarus but for us. Things are turned upside down from our old point of view, but the change is liberating. God makes all things new (Rev. 21:5).

Because the newness of life in Christ is a total newness, it is a sudden newness. There is no way we can gain it bit by bit. We cannot prepare for it; there is no way we can get from here to there by ourselves or find our own way to it. There is no way to the Way.

New life comes from beyond us and gives its integrity to us instead of developing from our integrity. When we live in the spirit of Jesus, our lives flow from a radically new source. So radically new in orientation are our lives in the presence of Jesus that, as I have indicated, they have been described from the time of Paul onward as being newly created. "Creation" so used means that there is no continuity from the old source of our lives to the new. There is only difference. Everything is gift; nothing is produced. Not just we are changed — the whole world is changed. We live in a world to which we can trust ourselves rather than living in a world within which we must defend ourselves. In the life of Jesus, the ultimate world of God's will enters and penetrates the immediate world of our lives so that we can live in that world with the security of God's will revealed to us. That is the personal world to which we belong and within which we are meant to be ourselves.

What I have just called the immediate world of our lives is the world in which we are our full selves as persons; it is the world in which we must recognize God if God is to make any real difference in our lives. It was with the reality of the world in which they spontaneously lived that the first disciples knew the reality of God in Jesus.

We are only too aware that the abstract thoughts we have about God do little for us as we are buffeted about in the reality of the world. Our faith is weak and our hope uncertain. We know effort but not joy in our religion; we experience doubt but not refreshment. Joy comes from victory, but for us religion is more apt to be a project requiring constant effort and work than a joyful celebration of victory. We spend ourselves trying to keep our fragile religious structures from coming unglued, rather than rejoicing in a gift of new life that liberates us and sets us free in the world.

How different our religious lives are from those of the first disciples. Their lives were expansive — not defensive — in the world. It was "so that our joy may be complete," according to the First Letter of John, that the Letter relates "what we have heard, what we have seen with our eyes, what we have looked at and touched with our hands, concerning the word of life." What was from the beginning, "the eternal life that was with the Father," was not just an idea or an inference that could be thought about in the world; the disciples believed it to be a person they lived with, actually saw and heard (1:1-4). How could such an immediate awareness of God's presence bring anything but joy to those who experienced it? Since we lack the concrete presence of God in our lives, is it surprising that our religion is weak and our lives are anxious? The reality of the world easily overpowers the reality of our religion.

Imagine the conviction that compelled the first Christians to live immediately with God in their daily lives. They felt that they had somehow seen, touched, and listened to God in Jesus. Their God could not be separated from their daily lives in the world, for they met their God only in their daily lives. That was the scandal of Christianity! That was why Jesus, after his resurrection, could no longer be regarded merely as a prophet or a teacher, even the greatest of prophets or teachers, and that was why he was regarded as more than a deliverer in the line of Moses. God did not stand behind Jesus or beyond Jesus, as God stood behind and beyond Moses and the prophets. God was not distant in Jesus' life; the mystery of God's life and the mystery of Jesus' life were one.

For Christian faith, God's life is found *in* Jesus. So immediately is God known in Jesus, the Christ, the one in whom the Spirit of God dwells, that the intimate presence of Jesus is discovered to be the intimate presence of God with us. Present with Jesus in the world, we know God's presence in the world; in Jesus, God's presence cannot be separated from the world. Those who knew Jesus felt they lived so intimately with the eternal life which was from the beginning — the life that was with God and that was God — that they had actually seen God with their eyes, touched God with their hands, and heard God with their ears.

In this way, God authenticated them and the world of their experience.

Our most immediate experience makes the most immediate difference in our lives. If our experience of God were immediate, God would make an immediate difference in our lives. The difficulty is that, unlike the experience of those recounted in the First Letter of John, our experience of the God in whom we believe is too remotely related to our lives. It may be claimed that God, by being God, is first in all things, including our lives, but the claim is an intellectual one. God's priority is only an intellectual priority; it has no place in the world of our seeing, hearing, touching, and tasting. God's priority is one that we admit in the world of ideas, but it is not an experiential awareness that orders our lives.

We live fleshly lives. The world of the flesh is the world spontaneously present to us, and in which, accordingly, we live with the least effort. We do not produce this world; we feel it produces us, for we arise and live within it. It is the world in which we appear — where we find ourselves to be ourselves and where we most fully express ourselves. It is a world into which we sink when we relax and in which we scrape our knee when we fall; in it we feel resistance to our heel when we walk; we are held up when we lie down. Even when — sometimes especially when — we are hurt in it, we feel at one with it. It is where we live.

The world in which we feel most ourselves is a world in which we touch and are touched. It is the world in which we show ourselves. Seeing, we want to be seen; hearing, we want to be heard. In this world the intensity of our lives is expressed both before and beyond words — by touch, action, glance — rather than being objectified by words. A word can never replace the squeeze of a hand secretly given when the word is spoken. The touch, not the word, is the precious thing we remember.

The world in which we meet each other is the world in which we must meet God, and that world, as I have been indicating, is the world of the flesh. We cannot think God into that world. We can think about God in that world, but we cannot think God *into* it. We cannot think ourselves into it either, for that matter. The world of objective concepts and intellectual analysis is different from the world in which we live and in which we are ourselves.

In scientific analysis, our everyday world is said to be a derivative world resulting from impersonal processes that have none of the characteristics of our immediate experience. The fullness and richness of our lives are absent from the world of science. The colors in a painting and the sounds of a symphony are reduced to wave frequencies; mechanics, chemistry, and molecular activity are held to account for our bodily movements and even the subjective feeling we have that we are agents controlling those movements. But is the world of our intellectual analysis the world in which we actually live?

An experience of Oliver Sacks, a professor of clinical neurology, well illustrates the difference between the world as it is intellectually conceived and the world in which we actually live — and it illustrates our inability to enter the world of our fleshly lives by thought alone. While mountain climbing on vacation in Norway, Dr. Sacks tripped on some loose rocks, fell, and found himself with his left leg twisted beneath him, limp and feelingless. Fortunately, he was rescued. In the course of his medical treatment and rehabilitation, however, he had to learn to walk again — which was no easy task, because the absence of feeling he first discovered in his leg at the time of the fall persisted. He could look down and see his leg still attached to his body, but he had no feeling that the leg he saw was his — that it was part of his body. It seemed strange and foreign to him. When the leg was strong enough so that he could begin putting weight on it again, he found he had to keep looking at the leg to control it; he had to think specifically at every moment precisely where he wanted the leg to go — in which direction and how far. That was the only way he could control the leg's movement. It was a leg, but it did not feel like his leg; external force rather than internal intention was the only means he had of controlling the strange limb he saw attached to his body.

As a neurologist, Dr. Sacks had an intellectual understanding of walking. He could analyze the process and describe the various muscular functions involved in it. He understood what needed to be done; he knew about the dynamics of walking, and he could see what he had to walk with. The difficulty was that he could not enter the world of his intellectual ideas and external vision. The world conveyed by his sight and his mind was different from and foreign to the world in which he lived. *He* could not get into it. There was no place for *him* in it.

The simple fact is that the world of our external observation and intellectual analysis is not the world in which we live. When Dr. Sacks tried to walk with the leg he saw beneath him but felt was not his own, he felt like he was walking with "a huge, clumsy prosthesis (or hypothesis), a bizarre appendage, a leg-shaped cylinder of chalk — a cylinder, moreover, which was still constantly altering, fluttering, in shape and size, as if I was operating a peculiarly clumsy, and unstable, robotic contraption, an absolutely ludicrous artificial leg."[1]

He began wondering if he would ever walk again with the spontaneity he had once known. And then came an unexpected transformation:

1. Sacks, *A Leg to Stand On* (New York: Harper Perennial, 1990), p. 144.

Suddenly — into the silence, the silent twittering of motionless frozen images — came music, glorious music, Mendelssohn, *fortissimo!* Joy, life, intoxicating movement! And, as suddenly, without thinking, without intending whatever, I found myself walking, easily-joyfully, *with* the music. . . . Suddenly, with no warning, no transition whatever, the leg felt alive, and real, and mine, its moment of actualization precisely consonant with the spontaneous quickening, walking and music. . . . All of a sudden, I remembered walking's natural, unconscious rhythm and melody; it came to me, suddenly, like remembering a once-familiar but long-forgotten tune, and it came hand-in-hand with the Mendelssohn rhythm and tune. There was an abrupt and absolute leap at the moment — not a process, not a transition, but a transilience — from the awkward, artificial, mechanical walking, of which every step had to be consciously counted, projected, and undertaken — to an unconscious, natural-graceful, musical movement.[2]

We cannot live our full lives in the fleshless world of ideas and geometrical color configurations. There is more to us and there is more to our world than that. We cannot be ourselves in an abstract world; we either walk out of such a world or find, as Dr. Sacks did, that we cannot walk into it. It just doesn't fit us; there is no way we can enter it. It is too thin.

For Sacks, it was music that entered into the impersonal world of intellectual phenomena and sensorial flashings. Continuing to stress the suddenness of the experience, he writes,

With no warning whatever, into the cold starry impersonal cosmos — the equally cold and impersonal micro-cosmos of the mind — came *music,* warm, vivid, alive, moving, personal. . . .

2. Sacks, *A Leg to Stand On,* pp. 144-45.

It was quintessentially quick — "the quickening art," as Kant had called it — quickening my soul, and with this my body, so that suddenly, spontaneously, I was quickened into motion, my own perceptual and kinetic melody, quickened into life by the inner life of the music. And in that moment, when the body became action, the leg, the flesh became quick and alive, the flesh became music, incarnate solid music. All of me, body and soul, became music in that moment. . . . Everything was transformed, absolutely, in that moment, in that leap from a cold fluttering and flashing to the warm stream of music, the stream of action, the stream of life. . . . An entirely new principle came into effect — what Leibniz called a "new *active* principle of unity" — a unity only present in, and given by, action. . . .

The phantasmagoria, the delirium, had no organization, no center. What appeared with the music was organization and center, and the organization and center of all action was an agency, an "I." What appeared in this moment transcended the physical, but instantly organized and reorganized it into a seamless perfect Whole. This new, hyper-physical principle was Grace. Grace, unbidden, appeared on the scene, became its center, transformed the scene. Grace entered, as Grace enters, at the very center of things, at its hidden innermost inaccessible center, and instantly coordinated, subordinated, all phenomena to itself. It made the next move obvious, certain, natural. Grace was the prerequisite and essence of all *doing*. . . . *Solvitur ambulando:* the only solution to the problem of walking is — walking. The only way to do it is — to do it.[3]

There is a striking similarity between Dr. Sacks' description of newly living in his wounded leg and the Christian experience of newly living in the world in Christ. The similarity must not

3. Sacks, *A Leg to Stand On,* pp. 148-50.

be overdrawn; nevertheless, there is much in Dr. Sacks' reliving the fleshly life of his leg that is comparable to and suggestive for religious living in our fleshly lives.

As Dr. Sacks wanted his leg newly animated, so we want the presence of God to animate our fleshly lives; and, just as Dr. Sacks recognized that his intellectual understanding of walking was not the same as his actual walking, so we find that our intellectual prescription for living with God is not the same as our actual living with God. We can think about walking, and we can think about God, but we can neither think ourselves into walking nor think ourselves into living with God. Both the walking and the living are activities beyond thought.

With the recalling of Mendelssohn's music, something different from his silent effort and thought entered Dr. Sacks' life. The "rhythm and tune" of the music, as he put it, broke into the silent, motionless world of ideas and frozen images. In an abrupt, absolute leap, the frozen world of ideas was warmed and quickened by the action of the music. I have noted Dr. Sacks' reference to the suddenness and spontaneity of the event: there was no process of transition. Suddenly there was a new presence — the presence of a wholeness, an activating and moving wholeness that incorporated Sacks into itself.

Action and spontaneity are the key to walking, just as they are the key to living. Sacks speaks of being "quickened into life by the inner life of the music"; his flesh became alive. Everything was changed absolutely and at once by the music; an entirely new unity had been given to his body by the movement of the music. Sacks appropriately describes the new unity his life received as grace, for "grace" means "gift." The quickening motion of the music was a gift of wholeness to him from beyond him; it was something already in action that incorporated him into its action.

From the time of Paul onward, the common Christian testimony is that life in Christ is also a totally transformed life,

[13]

absolutely different from life outside Christ. Our life in Christ is called a new creation because of the totality of its difference from our old life. The Christian life is not a partially changed life; it cannot be acquired bit by bit, piece by piece; it is a completely new way of living arising from a completely new source. It only comes at once as a whole; it is a life of grace because it is ours only as a gift from another.

As it was first lived and as it is truly lived, life in Christ is a fleshly life that can be seen, heard, touched, and felt. We need to know and live with God in the same worldly, fleshly manner as the disciples described in John's First Letter. If we felt God present with us as they felt God present with them in Jesus, wouldn't our lives be different? Totally different? Our lives in the world would change, and our lives would change the world. Our religious lives and the world would go together.

Abstract thoughts about God are incapable of making any difference in our lives, and the attempt to think and force ourselves into a new way of living — no more successful for us than for Dr. Sacks with his leg — is what keeps the practice of our religion joyless and the presence of our religion in the world inconsequential. It may be true to say that the way we practice religion keeps anything new from entering our lives in it.

As our religion becomes more and more asthenic, making less and less difference to us and no difference in the world, we ought to look again to Christian beginnings in the world. Could it be that we are missing something? Might it be that we are missing everything?

Our lives begin in the flesh; so did Christianity. We say the Word of God became flesh, and yet we have trouble getting our religion into our fleshly lives. The immediacy of God is not found in our most immediate lives in our most immediate world — all of which have to do with our lives in the flesh. Just as Dr. Sacks' fleshly leg needed to be newly quickened, nothing less than our fleshly lives have to be newly quickened if our religion is to make any real difference to us and give any real help to us.

Perhaps we have been looking for our religious quickening in the wrong place and trying to activate it the wrong way. We have learned some words, but we have ignored the full musicality of our faith. We have reduced the movement and action of music to frozen ideas. Christianity begins in movement; it begins in the fleshly life of Jesus. In his fleshly life he changed the fleshly lives of his disciples. Can he do the same for us?

If we let him come to us as he came to his first disciples, we may find that we can live with him as they did. Jesus comes to us walking so that we can walk with him; he comes to us in the action of his life to take us into that action. He comes not to tell us about God but to take us into the life of God. Just as walking is the only way to solve the problem of walking, so living with Jesus is the only way to solve the problem of living with Jesus. Jesus comes to share his life with us. There is nothing to know of Jesus but the dynamism of his life; the quickening of our lives by his life is his presence with us. Thus Paul wrote to the Corinthians that Jesus is for us "a life-giving spirit" (1 Cor. 15:45). Everything is moving, dynamic, spontaneous; nothing is frozen, static, calculated.

Our concern is to discern how the living Jesus makes himself known to us today — how we can today know the only Jesus there is, the living Jesus in the ongoing action of his life. It all begins in the life Jesus lived in the flesh — and in the life we live in the flesh. That is the life in which we need help, and that is the life to which help comes, if we will just receive the help God offers for what it is.

2

In the Face of Jesus Christ

THE WORLD in which we are most fully ourselves is the world of the flesh, and it is in that world that the presence of God will be of the most help to us. We are not able to think ourselves into the fleshly world; we find ourselves in it. Once we enter it, we can think about ourselves and about the world and about ourselves in the world. It is just that, as I have said, we cannot think ourselves into the world in the first place.

God would make the greatest difference in our lives if we could meet and recognize God in the world in the same manner that we meet and recognize the world and ourselves in it. We cannot "make" God operative in the world by our efforts, although the surreptitious attempt may have been made in the name of spiritual discipline from time to time, and, as we have seen, we cannot think God into the world of the flesh. It is God who has put us into the world, and if God wants us to know him with the reality of the world, God must make himself available to us in the world with that reality.

If God is going to "get into" our immediate lives with the reality of those lives, God must come to us in the same mode of reality as our lives. It is because Paul felt that that is exactly what

God did in Jesus of Nazareth that he wrote, "For it is the God who said, 'Let light shine out of darkness,' who has shone in our hearts to give the light of the knowledge of the glory of God in the face of Jesus Christ" (2 Cor. 4:6).

As I pointed out in Chapter One, our lives begin in the flesh, and so did Christianity. Jesus was born into the world as we are, and when we as Christians recognize Jesus to be the Christ, the only begotten Son of God, we see God in the world as we are in the world. It is because of the first disciples' conviction that they somehow saw, touched, heard, and lived with God when they saw, touched, heard, and lived with Jesus that the Letter to the Colossians speaks of Jesus as "the image of the invisible God" (1:15). That Jesus is the *image* of God means that he is the *appearance* of God in the world; in the life of Jesus, God's presence emerges in the world and has the reality of the world for us.

Christianity begins in the flesh, and it begins in movement: it begins in the movement of the fleshly life of Jesus. Those who recognized Jesus to be the Messiah saw him as the one sent into the world. He was in the world as we are, but once in the world he lived with a power, purpose, and success different from ours. Coming into our world, Christ lived in it in such a way that he changed it into his world, but the reality of the world he brings to us depends upon the reality of his entering our world in the first place. It is to the reality of his entering our world that we must now turn our attention.

We need to know God with the reality of the world, but what is the reality of the world?

The world — and here I use "world" as synonymous with "universe" — is an all-inclusive interrelation of activities and events. The ultimate reality of the world is the reality of events taking place, and, consequently, everything we know and do can be described in terms of the interrelations of events. So described, our lives are chains of events; when we come in contact with other people, the events constituting our lives intersect the events constituting their lives in a new event in both our lives. The world in which we live is a world of process.

Think of the process we go through in a developing friendship. We meet a number of people in the course of our lives. Some we meet only once or twice, and they and we pass on hardly influenced by our brief touching. There are some people we do not want to meet again, while there are others we not only want but try to meet again. When he is attracted to her across the room, you can bet he will arrange a more direct intersection of the events of their lives before the evening is over!

Because of our work, circumstances, or desire, we meet some people over and over again. As that happens, we begin bit by bit to know each other. To say that we begin to know each other means that, in the interactions we have with each other, consistencies begin to emerge over a period of time. We say that we learn what other people are like, which means that we learn what they like, how they use their time, and what they choose to do when they don't have anything they must do. Those who choose to use their time the way we choose to use our time are the people who become our friends. Free choices shared with another are the basis of the deepest friendship and love we can know. The wonderful thing about such a personal relationship is that there is no intrinsic reason why it should not go on forever. Sharing new, free acts of will describes a life of joy and fulfillment that could go on forever, and in fact it does describe the Christian understanding of everlasting life in the presence of God.

What we do and how we act are revelatory. Consistency in a person's actions and choices reveals the person's character. Our personality — the kind of person we are — is shown in our actions. Character and action go together. Neither is itself without the other, for each is revealed in the other.

Getting to know someone takes time, but that is the only

way our personal knowledge of one another can develop. Our lives, because they are strings of activities and events, are a way of using time. Being with a person during his or her use of time is the only way to be with that person. Because none of us can be separated from our use of time, someone who does not have time for us cannot be bothered with us. Not to like spending time with me is not to like me.

We need friends and companions with whom we can be ourselves as we spend time together; we need each other, and we can be our fullest selves only with each other. That does not mean, however, that everyone automatically has the type of friendship and companionship he or she needs. The so-called counseling professions offer a remedy for the situation: in them we pay someone to have time for us and spend time with us. A counseling session has cynically been described as buying friendship by the hour. The description is not fair, or course, because friendship cannot be bought, but the caricature at least offers an insight in its correlation of friendship with time.

One of the most frequent complaints we hear — and make — today is that there simply isn't enough time to get everything done that must get done. We attempt shortcuts both at work and at home, and we sometimes attempt shortcuts in our relations with each other. Some people are on a first-name basis with an astonishing number of other people, and it is commonly said that they have a lot of friends. Actually, there is a difference between being friendly and having a large number of friends. Aristotle said it was impossible, by definition, for one person to have a large number of friends, because friendship is based on sharing — ultimately, the sharing of time — and it is impossible for anyone to share the time that friendship requires with a large number of people. In earlier days, to be on a first-name basis with someone indicated that you were that person's friend. Casual acquaintances used formal modes of address, and only after two people had known each other for a considerable period of time — and then only by invitation — did each have the privilege of calling the other by his or her first name. Nowadays people feel that they have the right to call us by our first names when they first meet us — and often we feel flattered by the liberty taken. Conventions change, and there is something to be said for our relating informally rather than formally as soon as possible in our relations; on the other hand, a change in the social convention of address from a formal to an informal mode does not alter the nature of friendship itself. The ancient Greeks still have something important to tell us about friendship and the way we relate to each other as friends.

Calling people by their first names as soon as we meet them is an apparent shortcut in the exercise of friendship. A better shortcut is illustrated by conversation on a first date. Two people, physically and visually attracted to each other, want to get to know each other as quickly as possible. They have not spent time together, this being their first date, but because they desire to know each other as well as possible as soon as possible, what do they do? They spend their first time together talking about how they have used time before they got together. Talking about their interests and activities, they are excited to learn that they both like tennis, music, and the same kind of movies. The more they have in common, the more their future together looks promising. As many a disappointed lover knows, however, talk can be deceiving. It is possible to claim something that is not true and to be carried along by the desires of the moment. Is what a person says about himself or herself true? The other person can only know in time.

The danger in taking shortcuts in personal relations is the substitution of words for life. A shortcut on a date is appropriately called "making time." Words are substituted for reality. Something similar happens when we think of people solely as members of a class, a type, a race, a religion, a gender, or some other category. When we dismiss people this way, we do not have to take time with them. We project our prejudices onto them instead of learning who they are from them. Studies have shown, for example, that good-looking people are more quickly judged to be trustworthy than plainer people; immediate appearance is thus substituted for a person's action in time. We speak of a man's having been "deceived by a pretty face"; he wants to believe that "That's the girl for me." She truly is the object of his affection, but his future with her would be more assured if, instead of being the *object* of his affection, she were the *subject* whose decisions he had gotten to know over a period of time and whom he loved.

The significance of time and shared activity in human relationships can help us understand the difference between a painted portrait and a photograph of a person. What is the difference between a good painted portrait and a good photograph?

When an individual goes to a photographer to have his picture taken, he is scheduled for a sitting. At the sitting, the photographer takes a number of different pictures of him in different poses under different lighting conditions. The photographer subsequently submits a number of proofs to the individual, and from them he selects the one or two poses he likes best. The situation is quite different when an individual sits for a painted portrait; the painter does not submit a pile of pictures from which the subject chooses her favorite. In the course of sitting for a painted portrait, which lasts much longer than sitting for a photograph, the painter will no doubt ask his subject from time to time whether or not she thinks he has captured her mouth or her eyes or some other special feature. If she is not sure or says no, the painter will do some more work on the painting. Normally, more time will go into the painting, but not more than one painting will be produced. Photographs may pile up quickly, but paintings do not.

Similarly, we look at and judge photographs more quickly than paintings. It doesn't take us long to flip through a stack of someone else's vacation photographs, and we can even quickly flip through a pile of proofs from a photographic sitting, but we often have to study and contemplate a painting for some time before we are able to make a judgment about it.

We have noticed the quantitative difference between photographs and paintings: usually there are far more of the former than the latter, and the latter takes longer to produce. We have also noted that photographs, as a rule, are more quickly assessed than paintings. Let us now compare a single photograph with a single painting to see if there are additional differences between the two. Once again we will find that time makes a decisive difference.

Everything about a photograph is quick. We commonly refer to a photograph we take as a snapshot; it is taken in a snap. Not only is a photograph quick to take, but it normally offers a quick recognition of its subject. We can have a finished photograph in our hands almost as quickly as we can snap the shutter, and we can usually judge whether or not we like the photograph almost as quickly as we see it. When it is handed to us, a photograph is a finished product: everything that is going to be in it is already there. That's why we can usually tell at once whether we think the shot is a good one or not. Once we have taken our first look at the photograph, process is over — both of the production of the picture and of our perceiving the picture. When we look at a photograph, we are looking at a finished product.

On the other hand, when we look at a painted portrait, Maurice Merleau-Ponty points out, we are in a significantly different situation. We look at the portrait and ask ourselves, "Is it she or not?" We find it harder to judge the painting. A painting we did not like at first begins to grow on us, and the more we live with it, the more we find its living subject present with us. The process of discernment takes time. Why? Merleau-Ponty contends that our judgment of a painting takes time because there is something incomplete about the painting as it is presented to us. There is something we must supply to it.

Our looking at a portrait requires our participation in the painting in a manner that is unnecessary when we look at a photograph. A photograph has been completely developed by the time we see it. Not so with a painting. We partially develop the painting in our perception of it. When we look at it, we do not just passively observe what is already before us; we make a contribution to what we see.

Merleau-Ponty suggests that when we see the brush strokes of a painting, we are carried into the activity of the painter himself. Just as the painter took time with the picture, so we must take time with it. Merleau-Ponty goes on to claim that the time separating the artist's creation of the painting from our viewing of the painting is overcome in our perception of the painting: there is a sense in which we actually participate in the creation of the painting.

There is no doubt that we are closer to the texture of human life when we look at a painted portrait than when we look at a snapshot. We are more immediately involved in the action of life when we perceive the portrait than we are when we glance at a photo. We have a singular, personal relationship with a painting that we do not have with a photograph; we are in a human rather than a mechanical world.

I have been emphasizing the difference between snapshots and paintings, but it is important to acknowledge that not all photography is as mechanical and easily judged as a pile of vacation photographs. Photography can also be an art, and in its exercise, through the use of different lighting techniques and diffusion lenses, a viewer may participate in and complete a photograph much as a viewer does a painting.

If, instead of comparing a photograph with a painting, we

compare an obituary of someone in a newspaper with a painted portrait of that person, we can continue to gain insight into the nature of our personal relations with each other in the world of the flesh. An obituary is a brief biological sketch about a person, but a painted portrait makes the person present. Again we may ask why.

The facts mentioned in an obituary are true about a person whether he or she is dead or alive. "Facts" — a word coming from the past participle of *facio,* "to make" — are something made; in the case before us they are made by being abstracted from the events of the life of the person described. The recorded facts of a life are true whether or not the person in question is actually alive, but we all know there is a great personal difference between life and death. And the difference between an obituary and a painted portrait is the difference between an abstract chronology and living flesh! A portrait has an immediate relationship to the most intimate life of a person, for it is a representation of the person only as he or she is alive and enfleshed. Facts do not live; flesh does. After flesh dies, there is something radically different about it; it becomes no more than a body or a fleshless idea.

Look again at a painting. How does an artist reveal character? "Joviality," for example, is not a thing that can be painted. The simple fact is, as Merleau-Ponty points out, that "character" cannot be painted. An artist cannot paint an abstract concept, but an artist can paint a face in which we can discover joviality. It is not impossible for us to perceive the jovial nature of the person painted. The artist indicates the character of the person painted by using certain brush strokes, colors, and hues. The activity of the artist leads us to a perceptive experience during which we discover the joviality of the person painted. Sometimes we are not quite sure what is emerging, but, because the emerging is a perceptive process, we find ourselves engaged in the dynamism of the living person. We and the person painted live together, in

[25]

a sense, and it is the intrigue of the other person's liveliness that fascinates us.

How else can we describe the intrigue of the Mona Lisa's smile? It is often pointed out that she is just beginning to smile; her smile is something in process, not finished. We do not tire of looking at the Mona Lisa's picture, for it always suggests more than we actually see. Human life is a process, just as the perception of the portrait is a process. The life of the person painted and the perception of the viewer are of a kind; thus the life of the person painted is uniquely experienced by the person contemplating the painting.

I began this chapter by asking how God could enter our most immediate lives with the reality of those lives. The lives to which I refer are our fleshly lives, and I explored how we are present to each other in the flesh. In doing so, I described how people get to know each other and become friends, and I discussed our experience of another person's presence in our perception of a painted portrait. All of the relations discussed involve our lives in the flesh and the way we relate to each other in the flesh.

I also recalled the beginning of John's Gospel, in which we are told that the Word became flesh in order to dwell among us, and I recalled Paul's claim that it was the God who created the universe "who has shone in our hearts to give the light of the knowledge of the glory of God in the face of Jesus Christ" (2 Cor. 4:6). Everything fully human is incarnate; that is why, when God wanted to speak to us most fully, his Word became enfleshed, incarnate.

However, saying that God's Word became incarnate and dwelt among us does not in itself enable us to know God in Jesus as did the early disciples, who felt they saw, touched, heard, and lived with God in Jesus. The reality of the world that we see, hear, touch, and feel is the reality that I keep saying we need of God in the world, but how can that reality become our experience?

Too much of our knowledge of Jesus has the characteristics of an obituary or a finished photograph. Obituaries relate facts about people, but they do not make their subjects present. Certainly many of us claim to know a lot of "facts" about Jesus, but do we experience Jesus' actual presence in our lives by virtue of what we know? No one disputes the difference between knowing about a person and actually knowing a person.

It does not stretch analogy too far to claim that, although many of us have been presented a picture of Jesus during the course of our lives in the church, the picture presented to us has the characteristics we have discovered in a photograph. We have been handed a completely finished, instantly taken picture; everything is present in it at once; and even though we look at it, we have no sense of involvement with, or experience of, its subject. The picture of Jesus with which we are so often presented is something we look at but with which we feel no involvement. Jesus is someone we look at but do not live with.

We have seen that the world and our lives within the world are a web of interrelated events and activities. The world is a world of action and process. And we have seen that we are ourselves and that we know other persons only through the events and activities of our lives. Again, process is found to be the key to reality. Process, events, and activities all take time. For one reason or another, we sometimes run out of time, and when that happens, we try to take shortcuts to save time. When we attempt shortcuts in our relations with other people, we substitute an idea for a life, an abstract concept for living flesh. It is impossible to know another person instantly; persons are themselves only over time, and unless we can spend time with them we cannot be with them. Our basic perception of reality in our enfleshed lives is always a process, a forming that takes time.

The characteristics we have discovered about our lives in the flesh are important for our knowing God with the reality of those lives. What did it mean for Paul to say that God can be seen in the face of Jesus Christ? How were the disciples able to discern that it was God they saw, heard, touched, and lived with in Jesus? Can "God" be seen in Jesus' face? Can kindness be seen in a face? Can any characteristic be seen in a face? No one comes face to face with an idea, as Merleau-Ponty pointed out.

When we live with each other, the events of our lives inter-penetrate as we engage in common activities. The activities we share in time enable us to discover each other's choices, goals, purposes, and character. It is through the shared experience we have with another person that we eventually see the nature of that person in his or her face.

Only if we can participate in the actual life of Jesus can we see God in Jesus' face. Knowing about Jesus or picturing Jesus as someone who completed his life long ago will leave us total strangers to the only Jesus worth knowing — the resurrected, living Jesus. If God truly entered our world in Jesus to be with us in the first place, there would be no point to his having come if, once Jesus rose from the dead, God's presence to us in Jesus' life was removed from the world. Christian faith maintains that God still makes his enfleshed life available to us in our enfleshed lives. We should now at least have some intimation of what is involved in such availability.

3

How Fully We Are Accepted in Jesus

OLIVER SACKS' description of the quickening of his wounded leg, for all the suddenness and completeness of the leg's transformation, is the description of an essentially natural occurrence. Nothing in his account uniquely requires that the event have a supernatural dimension; everything he describes is "natural," the kind of thing that happens in the world of our fleshly lives.

Anyone who has ever tapped his foot, moved his head, kept beat with a finger, found himself or herself marching or dancing to a catchy rhythm knows that the movement of music can animate the static world of our thought. The best time for abstract thought or intellectual contemplation is not when a military band marches by! We know what Sacks means when he describes the movement of Mendelssohn's music becoming the movement of his body, which, in its transforming action, overcame the externality of his dangling leg. We know how music can lift our spirits, its thumping beat giving itself to our lives and moving us with it.

Sacks says that the "impersonal cosmos" to which his injured leg belonged became warm, alive, and personal by a new principle of unity that entered his life through the action of the music. What had previously been just an aggregation of sensory events and external observations he suddenly found to be a part of his life — organized, centered, and vivified by his renewed self. Instead of remaining the passive, helpless observer of his leg that he had been, he re-entered it and lived in it through the gift of the music. The liveliness of the music's tune and rhythm gave him spontaneity and movement; once he received that movement, it flowed through him from the "hidden innermost inaccessible center" of his being. Movement that he could not achieve by his effort he could receive as a gift.

In his description of the reanimation of his leg, Dr. Sacks offers no neurological or medical explanation of the event. In the medical profession, the account he gives would be called anecdotal rather than explanatory — meaning it is interesting but not medically helpful. It does not speak the language of medicine. Instead, it is a narrative account of something that happened; it offers no causal explanation of why or how it happened that can be abstracted from his experience, generalized for everyone, and prescribed for others as medical therapy. A religious person can see the will of God in the healing, but the recognition of God's will offers no possibility of laboratory testing on the basis of which God can be prescribed as a new therapeutic aid.

Of course, I am not trying to prove the existence and presence of God from Dr. Sacks' description of his healing. We come to the account of Dr. Sacks' healing in faith for reasons beyond his healing. Nevertheless, Sacks' description of the reanimation of his fleshly leg is significant for us, because it suggests the kind of difference and the level of difference God's presence should make in the world of our fleshly lives, if God really enters that world in the life of Jesus Christ.

I have said that Jesus was born into our world in order to change it into his world by the way he lived in it. The Christian claim is that the world centered in Jesus' life is the only world that lasts, a truth proved by the resurrection.

[30]

At the end of Matthew's Gospel, Jesus tells the eleven disciples that all authority in heaven and on earth has been given to him. It is with that authority that he will be with them (the Greek says "I am with you") all the days until the end of the age (Matt. 28:18-20). The Greek word translated "authority" in Jesus' statement is *exousia,* which literally means "from the being" or "essence" of something. So understood, the authority given to Jesus by God arises from Jesus' being sent from the Father to do the Father's will. Although born into our world, Jesus lives in it with a security from beyond it. The true being of a thing arises from the creative will of the Father, and it is the Father's will — the will Jesus came doing — that newly creates the world made available to us in the authority of Jesus' life.

Testifying before Pilate, Jesus said that he came into the world "to testify to the truth" (John 18:37). Born into the world, Jesus witnesses to the true source and nature of the world with the reality of the world. Having come from the Father doing the will of the Father, Jesus gives to the world newly created by his life the surety of God's almighty will.

That Jesus lived in the world of our flesh with his disciples, that he was born of a human mother and died on a cross to which he was nailed and upon which he bled, shows beyond doubt that Jesus lived and died in the world with the same reality we do. As I have indicated, the reality of Jesus' life in the flesh is the foundation stone of Christianity. Until we know Jesus with — and in — the reality of our fleshly lives, we have not yet *begun* to know Jesus.

Once Jesus was in the world as we are, those who knew him discovered that he lived in a mysteriously different way from anyone they had known before. He truly lived in a world different from theirs. Pointing out that difference was the purpose of Jesus' statement to those plotting against him: he said that they were "of the things below," while he is "of the things above" (John

8:23). The usual translation of the passage — "You are from below, I am from above" — while picturesque, does not quite catch the full meaning of the statement. Jesus lives differently in the world than do those who oppose him; the reality structuring his world differs from the reality structuring their world. That was also Paul's meaning when he described those living as enemies of the cross of Christ as having their minds set on earthly things: they preferred food to God, thus making their god their belly. They gloried in such living rather than letting their lives be transformed by the Spirit of Jesus, the one to whom all things are ultimately subjected (Phil. 3:18-21).

Since we all make personal worlds by the way we live in the world, Jesus rightly says that he is not of the world in which his opponents live. In John's Gospel, Jesus goes on to say that his persecutors will die in their sins "unless you believe that I am" (8:24). By saying "I am," Jesus identifies himself, his life, and the world centered in his life with the eternal being of God — the saving God whose name was revealed to Moses and the chosen people to be "I am" (Exod. 3:14). The presence of that God in Jesus' life is the source of Jesus' authority — and the source of the world Jesus newly created by his manner of living.

Returning to Matthew's Gospel, let us now consider Jesus' promise to his disciples to be with them all the days until the end of the age. Nothing truly Christian can be separated from the personal presence of Jesus, and, to the extent that we can experience Jesus' presence in our lives, we can experience everything Christian. That does not mean there is only Jesus; it means that, in Christian faith, God the Father can be known only through Jesus in the Spirit. That is why Christian prayer to the Father — to God — typically ends with the phrase "through Jesus Christ our Lord": Jesus is the door and the way to the Father, and wherever the risen Jesus is present, he is present as life-giving Spirit (cf. John 7, 9, 14:6; 1 Cor. 15:45).

Everything depends upon Jesus' presence in our lives, but how is he present with us now? It has been pointed out that even though the risen and glorified Jesus left this world, Jesus remains in the world in his Spirit, in his message, and in the ritual meal he instituted. If these are the means through which Jesus keeps his promise to be with his disciples day by day, none of the three can be itself if the living presence of Jesus is removed from it. More than that, since the living presence of Jesus is found in the gift of the Spirit, in his teaching, and in the commemorative meal he instituted, the essence of each is found in the other, for there is only one Jesus.

The Spirit is the source and moving principle of Jesus' life. In the mystery of God's trinitarian life revealed to us, the Father begets the Son and bestows the Spirit on the Son. By newly giving himself in the Spirit to the one begotten from him, the Father lovingly accepts the Son and rejoices in him. We are forced to use inadequate and distant language in trying to speak of God's inner life, but as Christians we believe that God has revealed his inner life to us in the life of Jesus. So it is that the help and the hope, the victory and the security, of the Christian life arise from Jesus' words in John's Gospel: "As the Father has loved me, so I have loved you; abide in my love" (15:9). In Jesus, God loves us as he eternally loves his only begotten Son.

The freest and most joyful way we accept each other as persons — and celebrate that acceptance — is in the offering and exchanging of gifts. When two people accept each other in marriage, that acceptance is commonly expressed in the giving and receiving of rings. Our acceptance by God is shown in the receiving of a gift also. In the dependency and insecurity of our lives, nothing could be more liberating than knowing that God embraces us and sustains us in his unfailing love. Because our being is insufficient in itself, both our future and our existence in the present depend upon all-sufficient being creating, accepting, and supporting us for who we are. The hope we have in Christ arises from the belief that, in Jesus, God comes to us to accept us and call us into the security of his life. God's accepting us in Jesus is achieved by Jesus' giving himself to us, ultimately bestowing on us the very gift of the Spirit that the Father bestows on the Son in the intimacy of their eternal life. By receiving, in the gift of the Spirit, the Father's acceptance of the Son in God's own life, we are accepted by the Father as he accepts his own Son. Only thus do we become, in the truest sense, children of God, for in Christ only do we live the life of God.

Certainly the Spirit of Jesus cannot be separated from the life of Jesus: where there is one there is the other. But what about Jesus' teaching? There are many people who talk and write fulsomely about Jesus' teaching but in whose lives we do not find the same fullness of Jesus' presence. Can Jesus' teaching be separated from his life — or our lives — and be itself? Not if the teaching is of the Jesus confessed by the church through the ages. Jesus' message is his life itself; Jesus taught by his life, for he is the *living* Word of God. The Word of God is a person, not an abstract word; abstract words can never substitute for a person. Jesus dictated no definitions to his disciples, but there is no doubt he taught others verbally when he talked with them and proclaimed the Good News. When early Christians orally passed on sayings attributed to Jesus or began to write them down in what eventually became the Gospels, they did not regard the sayings abstractly and conceptually. Words attributed to Jesus were "spirit and life," as John has Jesus put it (6:63), not letter and law, as Paul would contrast it.

There are ongoing disputes among scholars about which words, if any, in the Gospels are genuinely Jesus' words. There are few words or sayings about which there is overwhelming consensus that they came directly from Jesus' lips, but the lived and spoken testimony of others to the difference Jesus' life brought to their lives offers us genuine insight into Jesus' life. Since the essential message of the living Word is in the living, we do have reliable knowledge of the Son's witness to the Father.

There is overwhelming testimony that when Jesus did teach verbally, he taught primarily in parables — stories whose action involves the hearers' own decisions about what ought to be done in specific situations. These provocative stories may well have been based on stories common to the era; there is no reason why Jesus should not have used stories and illustrations common in his day. It is the common world that his presence changes, and the presence of the overall action of his life that is focused in the parables attributed to him makes the Gospel parables helpful to us whether or not they are Jesus' actual words.

The third means of Jesus' continuing presence with us in the world is in the ritual meal he instituted on the night in which he was betrayed. The Last Supper that Jesus celebrated with his disciples is associated with the Jewish passover and the deliverance of the Israelites from bondage in Egypt, but, just as Jesus is a different kind of deliverer than Moses, so the eucharist is different from the passover meal in the presence it conveys. Earlier I said that, because the presence of the living Jesus is found in the gift of the Spirit, in Jesus' message, and in the significance of the commemorative meal Jesus instituted, the essence of each is found in the other. Nevertheless, it can be said with good reason that the eucharist is, in a unique manner, the source, summary, and means of Christian living. Because of the holistic, summary nature of the eucharist, I will save our consideration of it until later chapters. When we consider it, it will not surprise us to learn that our concern will especially be the eucharist's relation to our fleshly lives in the world.

But first let us consider further the nature and significance of our acceptance by God in Jesus. I have spoken of the Father's acceptance of the Son in the gift of the Spirit, and I have said that, as we live in Christ, we are accepted in the Father's acceptance of the Son. To be accepted is to belong. The difficulties we have in the world can be described, in summary fashion, as *the* world not accepting us for who we are: it rejects the intentions of our worlds through its arbitrary disruption of them, and it finally rejects us in death. Considered in that light, God's accepting us in Jesus amounts to our being admitted into Jesus' world — a world whose mutual relations welcome, support, and nurture us rather than interrupting, threatening, and destroying us.

Our feeling of security with another comes from feeling accepted by the other. The insecurity we experience in our lives in the world spurs our search to find security somewhere. Ultimate security can be found only in God, the ultimate reality, but we must ask, What is involved in our allowing ourselves to be accepted fully by God? If God comes to accept us in Jesus, how can we accept the acceptance Jesus offers us? The answer to the question is found in letting ourselves be accepted by Jesus for who we really are. That, however, may not be as simple as it sounds. We may not know ourselves as well as we think we do, and, because of that fact, we may not expose our full selves to Jesus for acceptance. We may, knowingly or unknowingly, hold part of ourselves back from him.

Thinking about ourselves and reflecting on ourselves cannot give us adequate knowledge of ourselves. The selves we are in actuality are always more than the ego identity we have established in the past. Our egos are the selves we think ourselves to be; they are the objective way we see ourselves and conceive ourselves. But self-analysis does not necessarily yield self-knowledge. It has been said of the Sitwell circle of literati in London, for example, that, although they were most accomplished at self-analysis, they were most deficient in self-understanding. The same might be said of us. We often project our conscious appraisal of ourselves on ourselves. We accord what we call our intentions, but which are actually

abstract wishes, the status of the concrete action of our lives —
when, in reality, we never acted upon them. Our true intentions are
found only in our actions: an intention is an intention of an action,
and, if we do not perform the action, we never intended what we
call our intention. If I intend to make a $500 contribution to a
charity but never actually get around to giving the money, I never
really intended to give it; I only thought about giving it.

Our self-understanding is often our self-deception: the ego
image we hold of ourselves is often very different from the person
other people know. We defend ourselves by thinking that others
know us only by our external actions; we know our true intentions. Yet others may know us better than we know ourselves, for
the simple reason that we can be and become ourselves only with
others. What we dislike in ourselves may be something we
suppress in our consciousness of ourselves, only to act it out
unawares in our relations with others. The people with whom we
are most harsh are frequently the people most like ourselves; it is
much easier for me to condemn someone else's short temper than
my own.

The basic truth we must recognize about ourselves is that we
can know ourselves fully only in our actions — in our behavior,
in what we do. Who we really are is indicated by how we actually
live, not by what we abstractly think. The ego image almost
everyone has of himself or herself is grander than reality allows.
How often do we hear someone say, "He is not who he thinks
he is!"

Fully in Jesus' presence, we must be with him for who we
really are, not just for what we would like to think ourselves to
be or as we would like to present ourselves to him. To be fully
with Jesus, we have to be with him in all the things we have done
but would now like to forget — and even in the things we are so
embarrassed at having done that we say we were not ourselves
when we did them. Embarrassment after an act does not reduce

responsibility for the act. Actions we later regret were the way we were ourselves at the time we did them, for, as I have been saying, we are ourselves only in our actions. As selves, we are acting subjects, responsible agents revealing who we are in what we do. That is why we can know ourselves only in our actions.

Our temporal nature cannot be denied, for we are ourselves only in time as we use time. We can neither be ourselves nor know ourselves in an instant. We reveal who we are through the decisions we make during the course of our lives, and we, as well as others, discover who we are in the unfolding events of our lives. Our identity necessarily includes our past, for we have gone through the past to come to the present, but that does not mean we are completely determined by our past. Our past was once the future in which we became ourselves.

Without memory and continuity from the past, we have no self-identity, no sense of "I," but a human person is a subject that is open to the future as well as living in the present with his or her past. The future is beyond both the past and the present, and, if we will accept the newness the future offers us, that acceptance can change the effect of the past in our lives in the present. We can become more in the future than we were in the past; the past need not control our future.

Still, we must remember that the "I" which is called to become something new in the future includes its past. To want or expect to become a new self in an instant is to daydream. In such fantasy, we deny the reality we actually are, the reality of our past decisions. A "flight of fancy" is different from a genuine journey into the future. In the latter, nothing of us is left over or left out; in the former, we deny what we actually are in an empty wish to be what we are not.

Our true selves are always more than we have been. With the exception of only the most insecure and defensive people, we all admit that we should be more than we are; everyone has done things he or she regrets, and we have all left undone things we now wish we would have done. Those who try to be totally self-reliant in their lives and try to live only from their own resources must depend on no one beyond themselves to integrate and sustain their lives. The approval and acceptance of their lives must come from themselves alone. Consequently, if their actions ever become too much for their egos to handle, they must — if they are to maintain their integrity and self-approval — either find a way to block from their consciousness the previous actions of which they now disapprove, or find a way to blame others for them.

We can pretend to make our lives whole either by denial or by transference — or by a combination of the two: we can deny our responsibility for actions we have committed by transferring responsibility for them to others. When we employ such procedures, however, the wholeness of our lives is a false wholeness: we pretend that only what we wish to be is what we have been. We then try to substitute for the totality of our lives only that part which does not threaten our self-esteem.

We can fully accept and integrate the destructive and ego-threatening actions of our lives into the wholeness of our lives only if the strength by which we live comes from beyond us. The security given us by someone else who knows and accepts us in the deepest roots of our being — by someone, in other words, who accepts us at an even deeper level than our known or projected egos — is the gift we need to be set free from our past selves and to become more than those selves in the future. If we are secure in the acceptance of another, the smashing of our self-image by our past failures does not destroy our ability to acknowledge responsibility for the failures and to live beyond them. In such acceptance, another person truly gives us to ourselves — we acknowledge and become our full selves in the freedom of that gift.

To be accepted fully by another, we need to be accepted for more than our objectively and consciously known selves; we are more than our egos and more than our conscious awareness. Trying to live by our resources alone, as we have seen, we naturally avoid admitting more about ourselves than we can bear. Only in the assurance of unfailing acceptance by another do we find the strength to accept the full selves we have been — and only in that assurance do we have the strength to become the full selves we can be.

Dr. Sacks spoke of being activated by a new source of movement deep within the center of his being. He felt he had become a new self, and that is exactly how a Christian feels about himself or herself in Christ. Jesus accepts us for more than we know ourselves to be. Because Jesus is the creative Word of God made flesh, Jesus' acceptance of us on the cross is God's acceptance of us — an acceptance of us that is, paradoxically, deeper than our own being, for Jesus accepts us with and in the creative love from which we arise.

Knowing I am accepted by God in Jesus in the deepest roots of my being, accepted at an even deeper level than my conscious awareness of myself, I am newly able to accept my conscious life as a gift from Another. In the gift of myself I then realize myself to be, I am liberated from the need to protect and defend myself as my first stance in relations with others. Because my life and my security are given to me, they are not things of mine I need to defend. They are gifts I can share with others.

Living in Christ, we become new selves. Everything is different. We are given a total change of consciousness. Security arises from the deep, interior center of our lives; it is not something for which we must search in the world or something we must try to use the world to achieve. When we live our acceptance in our creating God, God's security provides the channel bed and direction within which our conscious lives flow. Our security arises within the center of our being, but it is not from us; it arises from an ultimate source more than and deeper than ourselves, to which we can commit ourselves if we will.

Commitment and security are essential to our lives. On the whole, it appears that commitment comes easier to us than security. Our commitments show in the decisions we make, and the decisions of people whose actions are reported in our newspapers and news programs indicate that, from individuals to nations, no commitment equals our commitment to ourselves. The difficulty is, as the news flashed before our eyes and flooding our ears testifies, commitment to ourselves does not offer much security. How could it, we being the fragile and dependent creatures we are?

Desiring security is one thing, but knowing what kind of security we need is another. In the quest for security that constitutes our lives, nothing is more helpful to us than first knowing who and what we are: not only in medicine is it true that proper diagnosis is a prerequisite to proper prescription. If, through ignorance or neglect of ourselves, we live partial lives, we must not be surprised that we never experience more than partial security in those lives. There is no need to belabor the often-made point that there will always be uneasiness in our lives until we live in the wholeness of our being. The lack of security that many people experience in the anxiety and fear of their lives may well result from just such an attempt to live with only a partial awareness of themselves rather than a full awareness.

When people worry about themselves, they are concerned about who they are. Many do examine themselves and analyze themselves; self-help books are major best-sellers and fill large sections of our bookstores. But as any number of the people who buy those books can testify, thinking about our lives is different from living them. The description "paralysis by analysis" holds for individuals as well as for groups and organizations. Only to think holds back action.

I have already indicated my view that ultimate security can be found only in the ultimate reality, God. It is not impossible for someone to think his or her way to that same conclusion, and it is not impossible for someone, once he or she has reached the conclusion, to spend additional time thinking about his or her life in relation to God. A friend with whom I have corresponded, and with whom I have discussed some of the problems of religion and believing in God over the years, once wrote that, in the midst of his constant thinking, he was becoming more and more convinced that a time comes when one must stop thinking. With that remark my friend did not announce his decision to abandon reason; the insight he had reached was that he could be his full self with God only by moving beyond abstract thought to a fully living relation with God. Life is doing, not thinking.

Special dangers arise if we try to relate to God in our thought alone. Because we can think only with our own resources, the constant approach to God through our resources and the constant expending of our energy on God subtly begin to subjugate God to our resources and to our energy. God becomes nothing but *our* problem; there is nothing in our relationship with God that God can do or originate without us. The result is that God can do nothing *for* us; who in his right mind would expect a god who is nothing but our problem to be an adequate source of our security?

At this point let us turn matters upside down and ask a question: Is it possible that the problems we have in our relations with God might originate in us rather than in God? Is it possible that the reason we are afraid to commit ourselves to God and the reason we can find no security in God are that we so restrict our knowledge of ourselves and of God to our analysis that we truly recognize neither our full selves nor an independent God? Perhaps there is something about both God and us left over in our conscious analysis of each.

The action of our lives, like a spring, flows up and over the threshold of consciousness from beneath the surface. If we acknowledge that the dynamic center of our lives as acting selves lies beneath the level of our consciousness, we may be able to live our lives — even with all their problems — with the wholeness of that source, rather than depending on the partial security that derives from consciousness alone. Solutions we provide for our problems will never solve *all* of our problems, for, in our deepest spontaneity as selves, a dimension of us always stands beyond the problems we are working on. We must stand beyond anything in order to grasp it and be able to analyze it.

God is the ultimate source of our lives; it is God who loves us into existence by willing us to become the active agents we are. The action of God's love so imparted to us beneath the level of consciousness is the spring from which the ceaseless dynamism of our lives flows, revealing itself, at the highest level, in our responsible activity in the world. Within such an awareness of ourselves, we see our conscious activity to be but one dimension of God's primary and originating gift of us to ourselves. We are created by the action of God's will, not by God's intellectual contemplation. In the reality we are, the willed action of love precedes the contemplative reaction of thought in our lives. In fact, that priority holds for the whole created order and accounts for the fact that reality created by God exists before, around, within, and after us, independently of our conscious thought about it. Our consciousness is not the source of reality — of our reality, the world's, or God's.

So realizing the fullness of our being in the fullness of reality — both as God's gifts — we come to the lived realization that we can commit ourselves to God and experience God's security in our lives even while some of the conscious problems we have about God remain unresolved. In the lived assurance that God loves and accepts us beneath the level of our conscious problems, we find that God's presence in our lives gives us, at once, the strength to address our problems and the strength to live with a security beyond them.

4

Sacrifice Turned Upside Down

MARK, MATTHEW, AND LUKE all recount an action of Jesus for which he was severely criticized by the Pharisees (Mark 2:13-17; Matt. 9:9-13; Luke 5:27-32). Walking by the sea one day, Jesus saw a tax collector, whose name was Levi, sitting at his tax booth. Upon seeing him, Jesus told Levi (who is also called Matthew) to follow him, which, we are told, Levi immediately did. Later in the day Levi gave what was apparently a large dinner for Jesus at his house. During the meal, Jesus and his disciples reclined and ate with other tax collectors and additional people who were known to be sinners — something that scandalized the Pharisees who observed the proceedings. They believed that no righteous person would associate with such people, and they asked Jesus' disciples why Jesus did such a thing. When Jesus heard the questions being asked, he responded, with minor variations in the three accounts, that he had come to call not the righteous but sinners to repentance; he came not to those who were well but to those who were sick. Jesus was where he wanted to be, and it was his "real presence" with sinners at the meal he initiated, by calling Levi to follow him, that scandalized the orthodox onlookers.

In Matthew's recounting of the incident, Jesus went on to say, "Go and learn what this means, 'I desire mercy, not sacrifice'" (9:13). The quotation is from Hosea 6:6: "For I desire steadfast love and not sacrifice, the knowledge of God rather than burnt offerings." The passage from Hosea is quoted again in Matthew 12:7; in this instance, Jesus' disciples picked some heads of wheat to eat because they were hungry. Even that slight act violated the work prohibition of the Sabbath, and the Pharisees were offended at that breach of righteousness also. Jesus, criticizing the critics, said in response to them, "But if you had known what this means, 'I desire mercy and not sacrifice,' you would not have condemned the guiltless."

It is in Matthew's Gospel that Jesus says that all the law and the prophets depend upon the double commandment to love God with all one's heart and soul and mind, and to love one's neighbor as oneself (22:36-40). According to Jesus, love rather than law is the singular basis of righteousness. Jesus' conviction arises from a religious consciousness that is the opposite of the religious consciousness of the Pharisees, because it removes all measurement and proportion from our relations with God and with each other in God's name.

It is the purpose of law to state and measure responsibility in relations between persons. During Jesus' time, the law specified and defined duties in relations with God — tithing practices and purification rites, for example — whose fulfillment could be judged by oneself and others. If the letter of the law were followed, perfection in righteousness could justly be claimed. On the other hand, there is no proportion to love; if one truly loves, one can never love too much — or enough, for that matter.

There is a world of difference between righteousness based on love and righteousness based on law, because the two perspectives structure two totally different worlds. The world centered in Jesus' life is a world of love and mercy, not of law and sacrifice;

Jesus eats with tax gatherers and sinners because the world of cult and regulation is turned upside down in his world. Jesus' world is a world of new gifts unmerited, not new rules required. Jesus' world is a world of mercy freely given, not balances restored.

Because we are a complex, interdependent system of systems as persons living in the world, our well-being requires proportion and balance both within us and in the world in which we live. We can neither think about nor tend to everything at once, so a homeostatic environment around us and a similar balance of activities and functions within us are necessary conditions for our lives. Cataclysmic variations either within us or in our environment destroy us. The destructive consequences of earthquakes, fire, and flood, of rage, revenge, and rape are well documented in human history. Balance and proportion describe the healthy condition of both individuals and societies.

It is the normative role of balance that allows us to determine excess. We all know the tendency to go to excess on occasion, and we all know the consequences we must suffer afterward until balance is restored. Many an enthusiastic drinker of the night before laments his excess the morning after; the advertising and weight-loss industries would lose a major portion of their revenue if multitudes of people did not purchase plans and pills to take off what they consider to be excess weight; too little sleep ruins our disposition and productivity the next day; not enough money keeps us from being the contented persons we would like to be; and inadequate recognition of our accomplishments shows how little knowledge and appreciation other people have of us according to our measure of ourselves.

Concepts of justice are especially concerned with proper proportion and balance. The goal of commercial justice is for the purchaser to receive equal value for the amount of money paid. Systems of justice are systems of reciprocity. Truly personal relationships are always reciprocal, moving in both directions between

[47]

the persons involved in them. The reciprocal relation in commercial justice, as I have just indicated, is the equal exchange of value for price. There are instances, however, when we feel that the equal treatment of everyone would be an injustice. Such a feeling accounts for the tradition of the sea that calls women and children into lifeboats first on a sinking ship. In the armed forces, everyone is expected to do his or her duty, but there are those who risk their lives or perform some service above and beyond that call. "Above and beyond" is a way of describing the exceeding of a measure; thus it is that exceeding achievement is thought to deserve recognition that exceeds a norm. Military decorations around the world recognize special achievements that range from stripes for length of service, through awards for marksmanship, to medals and citations for every imaginable feat of bravery.

"Everything in its place, and a place for everything" aphoristically describes the structure of justice that Plato prescribed for his Republic. It also describes the nature and role of religion in the course of human development. Cultural anthropologists supply us with evidence that primitive human beings experienced an affective coherence of all reality. They knew no distinction between the sacred and the profane; in terms of the distinction we make between the two, we would say our primitive ancestors experienced the sacred — a dynamic power or presence — diffused throughout all of nature. For ancient people, all reality was a coherent, sacred whole within which they lived and felt they belonged.

When, over the course of time, the sacred and the profane became separated, the role of religion was to re-establish the bond between them. The purpose of religious activity was to overcome the separation that had developed and to reintegrate human beings with the sacred; since they no longer discovered their lives within the sacred, the task of religion was to make human participation in the sacred possible. At the same time, a proper proportion had to be kept between the sacred and the profane, and sacrifice was accepted as the most effective means of mediating the separation and acknowledging the supremacy of the sacred.

The use of sacrifice to mediate the division between the sacred and the profane permeated the cultures of the eastern Mediterranean world of Jesus' day. R. K. Yerkes has discerned four purposes of sacrifice in the intercultural religious practices of the times. Sacrifice was a means of learning the will of God; it was a means of cooperating with God and doing his will; it acknowledged complete dependence upon God; and it could signify complete surrender to God. Yerkes suggests that it was precisely the richness and multivalent meaning of sacrifice that commended its use in describing the mediating role of Christ for us.

Jewish sacrifice emphasized the themes of offering, communion, and expiation. Elements of propitiation are also found in it, but the word *propitiation* is not much liked in contemporary theology because of the distasteful association with pagan sacrifices that were used to propitiate an angry god. Expiation is, accordingly, more acceptable, for it emphasizes cleansing and the removal of sin and guilt. Nevertheless, propitiation — taken in the sense of its Latin root, *prope,* meaning "near" — continues to offer a valuable insight into the nature of sacrifice.

The understanding of sacrifice as a means of drawing near to God is actually the oldest and most fundamental concept of Semitic sacrifice. In his book *The Religion of the Semites,* published in the first decade of this century, W. R. Smith showed that, for the Semites, the earliest significance of animal sacrifice — an older practice than vegetable sacrifice because hunting is an earlier human activity than farming — was not the slaying of an animal but the communal eating of it. Those who ate and drank together were friends and were mutually obligated to each other in their friendship. According to Smith, the earliest Semitic purpose of sacrifice was communion with a god. The killing of an animal was not the sacrifice offered; the killing was necessary only so that the animal could be shared at a meal. A god who admitted human beings to his table, at which the god and the worshipers partook of the consecrated animal together, admitted the worshipers to the god's friendship. Moreover, the act of communion binding the worshipers and the god together also bound the worshipers to each other. Animal sacrifice offered solely as a gift to a god was a later development, as was the development of burnt offerings in which the offering, completely consumed by fire, was wholly given to a god.

The received Christian tradition is that Jesus' death was a sacrifice for the sins of the world. In the letter to the Romans, Paul said that God did not spare his own Son, "but gave him up for all of us" (8:32); in his second letter to the Corinthians, Paul spoke of Jesus as the "one [who] has died for all" (5:14); the letter to the Hebrews states that "through the offering of the body of Jesus Christ once for all. . . . Christ had offered for all time a single sacrifice for sins" (10:10, 12). The letter to the Hebrews sees Jesus' death as the ultimate fulfillment of the Day of Atonement and interprets Jesus' death in terms of the ritual of that day.

On the Day of Atonement, two goats were chosen by lot; the first was killed on behalf of the people, and the second — the scapegoat, upon whose head was transferred the sins of the people through the laying on of hands by the high priest — was driven into the wilderness. Curiously enough, Hebrews never compares Jesus to the scapegoat, who actually bore the sins of the people; instead, the emphasis is placed on the shedding of blood and its significance for the inauguration of a new covenant. The Suffering Servant prophecies of Isaiah supply the major source of imagery for Jesus' bearing the sins of others, but there is no doubt that Hebrews sees Jesus' death as the fulfillment of the cleansing intended on the Day of Atonement because Jesus was both the high priest and the sacrificial victim of the day. There is also no doubt that in the Jewish understanding of atonement during Jesus' time, it was blood — which belonged especially to God — that was thought to cleanse from sin and bring about atonement.

When one reads the letter to the Hebrews today, one must remember that the letter was a communication addressed to a dissident group within a Christian congregation of Jewish converts. The faith of the dissidents had evidently been shaken, and they were apparently considering a return to Judaism. The letter, then, is a dissuasive communication written with a very specific purpose to a very specific group of people. Their background and their needs determined the vocabulary and structure of thought in which the author expressed himself to them. Because of the letter's inclusion in the New Testament canon, the letter has had a use and an exposure much wider than it was initially intended to have — and, while the letter's original intention was to liberate people for Christ, its ongoing effect has often been to restrict the liberation of Christ by forcing his life and death into a pre-Christian sacrificial mold.

While it is a commonplace to say that Christ fulfilled Old Testament expectation in a manner so complete that the fulfillment turned out to be beyond all expectation, it is almost as common to have the new wine of sacrificial understanding, arising out of Jesus' life and death, put into the wineskins of old thought forms. Jesus' admonition that new wine will burst old wineskins often appears to have no effect on contemporary homiletical and theological vintners.

The admission that Jesus shattered and redefined the understanding of the Law as the means to righteousness seems easier for people to make than the admission that he also shattered the understanding of sacrifice current in his day. Concepts of sacrifice current during Jesus' time were used to describe Jesus' mediating action between God and human beings because the concepts were at hand, but the meaning of sacrifice was turned upside down by Jesus' life, just as the meaning of Law had been. The new understanding of God given in God's revelation of himself should re-create our understanding of sacrifice; ancient understandings of sacrifice only limit our understanding of God's gift of himself to us in Jesus.

Much of the misunderstanding of the sacrificial nature of Jesus' life and death arises from the common Christian testimony that "Jesus died for our sins" (1 Cor. 15:3). In a significant manner, it can be said that everything Jesus did he did for us; for Christians believe that Jesus, the Son of God, was sent into the world by God to mediate and overcome the separation between God and his sinful creatures. But we do not get the whole picture if we simply say that Jesus died for us and nothing more. Granted that Jesus died for us, the question remains *how* he did so. Here is where we enter the picture and where we cannot be left out of the picture: Jesus died for us by dying by us. Human beings (we) are the ones who killed (kill) Jesus; if we look at Jesus' life and death as a one-person play God puts on for us, the action we observe will be that of God killing his Son. But would the God who has revealed himself to be love kill his Son? There are many who answer yes to that question, for they say the ultimate love God wanted to show was his love for us, and, in that love, he was willing to sacrifice his own Son.

It is true that Jesus was the sacrifice for our sins, but this is the primary instance in which "sacrifice" must not be equated with "killing." The willingness of Abraham to sacrifice his son Isaac is traditionally taken as the Old Testament anticipation of the consummating love that God revealed to us in sacrificing his only begotten Son for us. But the real point of the Old Testament story is that, although Abraham was willing to kill his son, God does not accept such sacrifice. God's providing the ram caught in the bushes, which Abraham saw when he raised his eyes, is God's prohibition of the kind of sacrifice Abraham was prepared to offer. In the revelation of Jesus Christ, God shows that the equation of sacrifice with death, immolation, or destruction is wrong in any form it may take. The Christian meaning of sacrifice, as we will see, is the doing of the will of God.

It is impossible to overestimate how difficult it is for us to receive the self-revelation of the God who is God because of his total difference from us. We are what we are, and whatever we know — even when we acknowledge its difference from us — must be accommodated to our abilities. Nowhere, however, is such accommodation more disastrous than in our relations with God. We are not ourselves unless we use all of our faculties, and in our mindful relations with God that means we will somehow have to know God by means of our thought forms.

Anselm was aware of this problem in the eleventh century, and his solution to the problem was based on his well-known dictum, *credo ut intelligam:* I believe so that I may understand. Accepting God's revelation in faith, Anselm then set about to understand, as best he could, what God had revealed and what that revelation meant for life in the world. The human need for balance and proportion, to which I have previously referred, has shown itself throughout the history of Christian theology in, among other things, distinguishing within God the two attributes of justice and mercy. The tension between justice and mercy is a constant source of anguish in our world: we generally say that justice should be tempered by mercy, but it is also commonly held that mercy should not destroy justice. The undeniable factor is that, in a system of balanced justice, mercy and justice are contrary to each other. How can we keep the proper balance between them? Although we have attributed both justice and mercy to God, God does not remove the tension we know between the two in the world; instead, the difficulties we have in the world we now have in God also. To be sure, God is a God of love and mercy, but God is also a God of justice.

Within the faith he accepted, Anselm reasonably resolved the problem of the relation of mercy to justice by what is known as the satisfaction theory of the atonement. In Anselm's view, creation was good upon delivery, but, by exercising their free will, human beings sinned against their creator. Justice requires that sin be punished and that some kind of recompense be made for offenses. Because human sin was an offense against the infinite God, justice requires that restitution be made in kind. The difficulty is that human beings have no resources with which to make restitution: they are finite, and everything they are and have already comes from God. Realizing their plight, God, who is merciful as well as just, sent his Son into the world to be the sacrifice for human sin, the infinite offering that humankind could not make. The rift that sin caused between human beings and God is thus overcome by God's mercy satisfying God's justice.

No one can fault Anselm for wanting to be reasonable in his belief. But we may nevertheless ask if Anselm was really being reasonable in his reasonableness about God. Although Anselm received the premises of his reasoning from faith, once he began to work with them we may ask whether or not he was consistent with them. Accepting, in faith, that the Father sent the Son into the world, Anselm constructed a reasonable and consistent argument claiming to explain *why* God sent his Son. Starting from premises that would be foolishness to the Greeks, as Paul puts it, Anselm ended with an argument the Greeks would respect about why God acted as he did. Paul's point was that, because God is totally different from us, God's foolishness remains foolishness wherever it is found. For all of the primacy that Anselm allowed faith, receiving God's revelation in faith did not shatter Anselm's old thought forms. It might be said that faith lifted human reason to a higher plane of operation, but once there, human reason remained itself and took over.

Anselm saw the problem of reconciling justice and mercy in

God in objective, quantified terms. Justice and mercy were objective principles in God that had to be proportionally balanced and respected. The equally eternal principles of justice and mercy in God required God to do what he did; otherwise, God would contradict himself.

Anselm acknowledged the scandal of Christianity, but the scandal was not so much God's difference from us as the quantitative excess by means of which God does what we do. For Anselm, the scandal of Christianity was not how differently God does business than we do, but the sums with which to do business God has at his disposal. In the reasonableness of Anselm's faith, God's difference from us is more quantitative than qualitative.

The scandal of Christianity is much more scandalous than Anselm could allow. The scandal of Christianity is that the God who is Love works by gift — pure, unadulterated gift. There is no reason for what God does other than love, and God's love arises from the totally free act of will he is. The Christian revelation is that Love is a Person and that nothing impersonal is found in God. God is the pure, spontaneous act of love; God's reason and will are one, which means there are no abstract principles within God to which he must bend his will.

The God of love is the God of gifts. Everything we receive from God is a gift, something we could not obtain by our own effort. A true gift is always totally new to the one who receives it; that is why gifts liberate us and exhilarate us — they *are* something for nothing! All we can do is enjoy them. Our lives can be completely changed only by new gifts to live *from;* new truths to live *by* continue to throw us back upon our own efforts.

Christianity is utopian. There is nothing else like it in the world; if we think the Christian life is a life we can live by our own efforts, it is too good to be true. The trouble with human utopias is that they suppose human beings can forget or deny their past and by themselves alone create a new future different from their past. There is no doubt that human beings are more than their past; the question is whether or not they can be different from their past if they draw only from their own resources. The convincing and unanimous answer of the whole of human history is that they cannot.

Doesn't the past show who we are in ourselves? We are our past while we listen to the call of the future, but if we have only ourselves to work with, where will any newness in the future come from? If we are left to ourselves alone, our desire for a new future is empty. We need to be called beyond ourselves. Anything truly new in our lives must be given to us; we must receive it as a gift and then live from it. If we are to create a new future — instead of only repeating the past — we must receive before we can act. Isn't action always inspired by something beyond itself? As human beings we can use what we are given, but we cannot create anything different from ourselves by ourselves. A truly new beginning in our lives is always a gift.

The scandal of Christianity turns the nature of sacrifice upside down: instead of God accepting us and our gifts, we have to accept God's gift to us. It is utopian from our point of view — more than, and different from, anything we can do; that is why it is our only true liberation. Sacrifice is a means of propitiation; it is a means of drawing near. But in the life and death of Jesus, God is the one who draws near to us; we are the ones propitiated! God did not will to kill his Son as a means of giving satisfaction for our sins, but God did freely will to send his Son to those who would kill him — so that they (we) could learn that love is always creative and initiating, never destructive and reactionary. In the crucifixion, Christ accepted the judgment of human beings; in the resurrection, Christ accepted the judgment of God! God so loved the world that he sent his Son to submit to the judgment of the world, to enable the world to know what its ego-directed power does (it kills) and what God's other-directed power does (it gives life).

The anger propitiated in the death of Christ is ours, not God's. God propitiates us in Jesus by giving himself to our will. God overcomes the "judicial character" of human beings by totally accepting such judgment in Jesus; in so doing, God shows what the ultimate outcome of human, ego-centered judgment is: conflict, abandonment, condemnation, negation, isolation, death. Having totally accepted human judgment of God's will in the death of Jesus, God overcomes the judgment of death with his judgment of life. God's justice is the resurrection — God's continual giving of himself, and in that judgment, God in his love destroys all categorical, abstract systems of justice that are less than love.

The resurrection of Jesus from the dead shows that God's last Word, like his first Word, is creative love. The creativity of love can never be defeated. For that reason, love is able to win final victory without ceasing to be itself. It does not have to become like its enemy to defeat its enemy. Instead, it remains its accepting self and lets others judge themselves by their actions. Love, instead of destroying its destroyers in retribution, seeks to redeem even its enemies by remaining different from them and showing them that, in the end, there is no alternative to itself. It is in the security of such Love that Jesus accepts the consequences of our acts into himself so that we can accept them in him — which means we accept him instead of them. In Christ we can admit and accept our past, and, when we live by the strength of Jesus in order to acknowledge our past, we experience his love as the gift of our new future already in our lives.

The Letter to the Hebrews, for all of its references to the Day of Atonement and its assumption of the Jewish sacrificial system, sees Jesus as inaugurating a new relationship between God and human beings in which such sacrifices are abolished. The Letter

makes its point by saying that, in Jesus, the assertion of Psalm
40:6-8 is fully achieved. Those verses, in the form used in Hebrews, read as follows:

> Sacrifices and offerings you have not desired,
>   but a body you have prepared for me;
> in burnt offerings and sin offerings
>   you have taken no pleasure.
> Then I said, "See, God, I have come to do your will,
>   O God"
> (in the scroll of the book it is written of me).
>
> (10:5-7)

Attributing the quotation from the Psalm to Christ, the letter
continues: "When he said above, 'You have neither desired nor
taken pleasure in sacrifices and offerings and burnt offerings and
sin offerings' (these are offered according to the law), then he
added, 'See, I have come to do your will.' He abolishes the first
in order to establish the second. And it is by God's will that we
have been sanctified through the offering of the body of Jesus
Christ once for all" (10:8-10).

For all of the references in Hebrews to blood and the removal
of sin by blood, the Letter finds the effectiveness of Christ's
sacrifice in Christ's obedience to the will of God rather than in
the shedding of his blood. According to the Letter, Christ
abolished the old order of sacrifices and offerings by establishing
a new relationship of the human will with God. The Christian
meaning of sacrifice, as I indicated, is found in the doing of God's
will, not in the killing or destruction of a victim. The Greek word
for sacrifice, *thysia,* basically means "an offering." The Latin word
sacrificium comes from the two words *sacrum facere,* which mean
"to make sacred" or "to do the sacred." Louis Bouyer has pointed
out that, strictly speaking, human beings cannot make anything

sacred. To do so would be to control God. Accordingly, Bouyer concludes that the most primitive and the truly essential nature of sacrifice is the doing, rather than the making, of the sacred. A liturgical sacrifice is an action or service through which human beings hand themselves over and submit themselves to the will of God.[1] According to Bouyer, such a communal agreement of wills is pre-eminently found in a sacred meal. We thus find ourselves again at the earliest Semitic understanding of sacrifice: communion with God. "To sacrifice" is "to do the will of God," and doing the will of God is eminently celebrated at the table of God.

The offering of a sacrifice is the offering of our will to God. That is how we do the sacred. "To sacrifice" is to live according to God's will; it is not to kill something in God's name. If "sacrifice" meant "to kill" or "to destroy," it is difficult to understand how Paul could write to the Romans, "I appeal to you, therefore, brothers and sisters, by the mercies of God, to present your bodies as a living sacrifice, holy and acceptable to God, which is your spiritual worship" (Rom. 12:1). Paul wasn't telling the Romans to go out and kill themselves!

The sacrifice of Jesus is his whole life of obedience to the will of the Father. The sacrifice of Jesus' life culminated in his death and resurrection, but his sacrifice for us was his whole life of witness, not just his death. Jesus' witnessing to the will of the Father led to Jesus being put to death by those who opposed God's will, but the death of Jesus was not what the Father willed as a sacrifice to himself. The Father is Love, and Love wills only life and resurrection. That was the witness of Jesus.

1. See Bouyer, *Rite and Man: Natural Sacredness and Christian Liturgy*, trans. M. Joseph Costelloe, S.J. (Notre Dame: University of Notre Dame Press, 1963), p. 82.

5

The Scandal of Mercy

ONE OF THE most scandalous aspects of Christianity is its having turned upside down the prevalent view of sacrifice in Jesus' day. In Christian sacrifice, we accept God's gift to us rather than God accepting our gifts to him.

It is difficult to live the Christian life, but the difficulty is one of accepting rather than doing. No one becomes Christian by self-effort from a dead start. Christian doing depends upon the acceptance of something prior to it, and it is there, in the beginning, that the characteristic difficulties of Christian living are found.

The liberation we know in Christ arises from the paradoxical truth that, in Jesus, God's acceptance of us is deeper than our own being. God, in sending his Son to us and accepting us in his Son, accepts us in the creative love from which our being springs. In that love, God loves us not just as we are in the present, but in his will for us before we were created and in his will for us in the future beyond the present.

In Jesus, God accepts us for we what we are now, but not just for what we are but for what he can give us in the future. God bestows upon us the gift of his acceptance now so that, if we accept his gift, he will be able to give us more in the future. Judgment is involved in such giving and receiving, but the only restraining judgment is ours, not God's. How much of God's love we will accept, not how much God will love, is the question. Judgments of condemnation are always judgments we make about ourselves; they are never God's judgment of us. God always offers the gift of himself — which is to say, God always offers his love — to us; it is our refusal of God, not God's refusal of us, that condemns us to the death of isolation from God. Difficulties between persons ultimately arise from conflicts of will. So it is in our relations with God: our wills contradict God's will. The turning of sacrifice and sacrificial living from "gift receiving" and "joyful communion" to "destruction" and "painful giving" is a case in point.

"To sacrifice," we have seen, is "to do the sacred" — to do God's will. When we hear of someone who has sacrificed himself or herself for a cause or for another person, we normally take the statement to mean that the person has given up what he or she really wanted to do and would rather have done. Going against one's feeling is precisely what makes the action "sacrificial." Sacrificial giving means to give until it hurts.

On such a view, we live sacrificially with God only by reluctantly submitting our wills to God's will. Some say "No pain, no gain" when it comes to physical exercise; similarly, plenty of spiritual exercises can be found that are painful enough to offer considerable gain to those who will undertake them.

The truth of the matter is that God does not force us to do his will. God does not overpower us. Witness the death of Jesus. God did not will Jesus' death, but God did not prevent us from killing his Son. If God achieved victory by force rather than by mercy and love, those who submitted to him would be losers, not victors. And that is, in fact, the opinion of the world about the disciples of Jesus: in the eyes of the world, "humility" is a synonym for "weakness"; worldly strength shows itself in domination. A God whose almighty power is shown in mercy is scandalous.

If God makes converts by overpowering them, Christian discipleship is but another instance of life with God differing from life in the world only by the quantity of force involved. Just as a big army can defeat a little army, so God's big Will can defeat our little wills. To be saved is to be subdued.

The true losers in the world are those who cannot do what they want to do. Slaves are those who must do the will of another. Paul called himself a slave of Christ, but, because Paul's God is love, Paul was a slave by choice rather than someone enslaved by force. Love is itself only as an act of free will: a lover makes himself the slave of his beloved by his love for the beloved. Such slavery is the lover's fulfillment and source of joy, not the lover's defeat and regret.

Doing God's will is not the following of a law for fear of what will happen if the law is broken. Drivers may observe speed limits for that reason, but it is not the reason that Christians do the will of God. God does not "lay down the law" to us and then externally achieve our compliance with his law by external force or fear, the way police and the fear of being arrested are used to enforce traffic laws. God, instead of giving us a law to be fulfilled and lived by, offers to give us a fulfillment so great that it could never be commanded! God gives us himself — not a restriction about ourselves and our lives. As it is commonly put, instead of giving us a new law in the life of Jesus, God gives the moving Spirit of Jesus' life to us. Christianity is a religion of the Spirit, not of law.

We may now see the significance of Jesus' remark to Thomas, "I am the way, and the truth, and the life" (John 14:6). When Jesus said that he is *the* truth, he was saying that he is not a truth to live *by*. That is, Jesus is not, and cannot be reduced to, an abstract rule or principle that we are left to apply to our lives as we are able. Jesus is not an abstract truth about which we can take the initiative. Jesus takes the initiative and comes to us. In his coming, the action of his life is given to us in its action, and it is only as we are incorporated into that action that we live with Jesus. There is a significant sense in which we can live *in* Jesus and *with* Jesus, but there is no way we can live *by* Jesus.

When Jesus says that he is the way, he indicates that he does not point *to* a way. Jesus does not point to something beyond himself or separate from himself that others may use by themselves. There is no way to God without Jesus. Jesus' presence is *the* way because his presence *is* the goal! Christians find the life of God in Jesus, and that life is our goal. Jesus alone offers his presence to us by coming to us; no one by himself or herself can make or discover that presence. Thus, the way to God — the way to do and live the sacred — is the sole gift of Jesus to us.

Just as Jesus said that he is the truth and the way, he also said that he is the life. Jesus' life is not just a life; it *is* life, the only life. If we are truly to live, our lives must not be like Jesus' life — his life must be our life. Paul may tell others to be imitators of him (1 Cor. 4:16), but no one, neither Paul nor we, can imitate Jesus' life. In another passage in First Corinthians, Paul tells those to whom he is writing to "be imitators of me, as I am of Christ" (11:1). But there is nothing Paul said that we can feel more assuredly he did not mean than this slip of the pen, for no one has emphasized more consistently than Paul our need to be baptized *into* Christ, and no one has emphasized more than Paul that the Christian life is life *in* Christ, not life outside of Christ trying to copy him at a distance. Paul's firm belief and conviction are found in his letter to the Galatians, when he writes that "it is no longer I who live, but it is Christ who lives in me" (2:20). Paul does not think we can imitate Christ by our own efforts. Jesus' life is singularly and uniquely God's life. That is the only genuine life there is; anything else is an imitation whose imitative nature is proved by the grave.

God's will does not become our will until we want to do it; God's will is our will only when we freely desire to do it and find the joy of self-fulfillment in doing it. We can do God's will only if we first accept God's gift. In that gift everything is changed; we are liberated from our efforts and freed from dependence upon ourselves. That is how Christianity turns the nature of sacrifice — of doing the sacred — around. To sacrifice by our effort is to give up and to lose. Such sacrificial giving does hurt. But when sacrifice first of all becomes our acceptance of God's gift of himself to us, sacrifice, instead of being our loss and deprivation, is our communion and friendship with God. Christian sacrifice is not a victory for God achieved by our defeat; it is God's accepting us as his friends and his sharing of himself with us. In sacrifice, God has nothing to prove — only something to give!

There is a great difference between the power of unlimited love that can never be exhausted and limited power that cannot afford to squander itself. We can give only what our resources allow, and what parent has not said, when turning out the lights in an unused room or looking at unexpected bills, "Do you think I'm made of money?" God, on the other hand, *is* love. God does not run out of love, and his love is never defeated. Those truths should be our ultimate comfort, but in a fallen world they are the ultimate threat to our concepts of justice and proportion. If God loves everyone and if God wills that everyone be saved, no one will be damned. Why then should we behave? Are there no moral standards; is there no moral restraint? If everyone is going to be saved, anything goes!

The view that everyone will finally be saved is called universalism. It has been around, here and there, through the Christian centuries, but it has never been the primary Christian proclamation. It is easy to understand why that has been the case: people oppose universalism because they feel it makes some — usually themselves — losers. A religious loser is a person who does not really want to do God's will, but, because of fear of punishment, manages to avoid the most obvious sins — or at least avoids sinning obviously. What is worse than feeling obliged to do something you don't want to do and then finding, after you have denied yourself, that those who didn't restrain themselves get the same benefits you do? If I go to a class at which attendance is being kept because I don't want to be punished for my absence, and a friend of mine who skipped class and was reported absent isn't punished, I feel I am the victim of injustice. I lost by doing the right thing. I had wanted to skip class too. If universalism is true, does that mean that everyone who tries to do the right thing in the world is a loser?

Universalism actually means that no one is a loser — even those who try to behave and do what is right. Universalism is not the name of an abstract principle that is impersonally applied to all — giving the same reward to the just and the unjust alike. Rather than conceiving of universalism as a principle, we would do better to think of it as the universal application of a loving relationship between persons. It could well be thought of as the universal application of the parable of the prodigal son.

The parable of the prodigal son is frequently said to be the favorite Christian parable. Men and women through the centuries have seen themselves as the prodigal returning to God, their Father. We do not mind the parable when we see ourselves as the returning younger son, but our sense of justice still makes us chafe if we see ourselves in the role of the older son. We feel cheated, as he did, by the undeserved reward given to the wayward son.

The parable of the prodigal is so well known that there is no need to recount it in detail, but we do have to look at its structure in the light of our discussion (Luke 15:11-32). After the younger son had taken the property which was to be his inheritance, left the country, and spent all of his money on riotous living, we read that, after he had hired himself out just to stay alive, "he came to himself" (v. 17). The father did not judge the son; having to live the consequences of his own decisions was the judgment the younger son made of himself. When the younger son finally came to himself, his sense of justice made him realize that he had no claim left on his father, but he nevertheless returned to his father, hoping at least to get sustenance and a place to stay in exchange for his work, as would any slave or hired hand.

As the younger son was returning home, his father saw him in the distance and "was filled with compassion" (v. 20). He ran out to meet his son and embraced him and kissed him. Bernard Brandon Scott points out that, by so lavishly greeting his son, the father violated the honor and character of an eastern master or patron.[1] In his enthusiastic and affirmative reception of his son, the father turned the legal and paternal roles of his day upside down. The father then ordered his slaves to bring out the best robe for his son, which, Scott suggests, would have to be the robe of the father himself. By so doing, the father put the younger son in a position equal to his own. The younger son's acceptance was complete.

The father may have violated the code of honor and justice of his day by welcoming his younger son home in such an exaggerated fashion, but the elder son still knew and lived by what was proper and right. The clue to the older son's indignation is found in his remark that he had worked like a slave for his father and had never disobeyed his father's command. The elder son saw himself as properly subservient and submissive to his father, no doubt doing what his father wanted him to do when

---

1. Scott, *Hear Then the Parable: A Commentary on the Parables of Jesus* (Minneapolis: Fortress Press, 1990), p. 117.

he, the son, wanted to do something else. When the father heard this, he told his elder son that, in his eyes, the elder son was not a dependent slave but a co-owner and companion with the father in everything he had. The words of the father are, "Son, you are always with me, and all that is mine is yours" (v. 31). Because the father and the elder son shared all things, they had to celebrate and share together the joy of the one who "was dead and has come to life," the one who "was lost and has been found" (v. 32).

Understanding the parable to be a parable of the kingdom, Scott states that the parable "subverts the myththeme by which the kingdom decides between the chosen and [the] rejected. Here the father rejects no one; both are chosen. . . . In the parable the kingdom is not something that decides between but something that unifies. The father does not reject. The metaphor for the kingdom is the father's coming out, both for the younger son and for the elder. . . . The kingdom is universal, not particularist."[2]

Other parables of the kingdom make the same point: entrance into the kingdom depends not upon proportional justice and hard work but upon a freely bestowed gift and mercy. In the parable of the landowner who hired laborers for his vineyard, we read that he hired workers early in the morning, at about nine o'clock in the morning, at noon, at about three o'clock in the afternoon, and lastly at about five o'clock. The landowner negotiated a wage with the first workers he hired, and said (or implied) to the other workers that he would give them whatever was right (Matt. 20:1-16). At the end of the day, when the workers were called together to receive their pay, the workers who had labored shorter periods of time received the full daily wage negotiated with the workers hired early in the morning; the scandal was that those who had worked a full day received only what they

2. Scott, *Hear Then the Parable*, p. 125.

had agreed to. Such an obvious injustice caused the first workers hired to complain. The parable is brought to a conclusion with the landowner's asking those who were first hired, "Are you envious because I am generous?" (v. 15), and with this summary statement: "So the last will be first, and the first will be last" (v. 16).

Scott sees the parable as underscoring precisely the themes we have been discussing. "The lack in the parable of any absolute standard of justice," he states, "undermines any human standard for the kingdom. For the parable, value or worth (i.e., a place in the kingdom) is determined not by what is right but by acceptance."[3] Comparing the vineyard to the kingdom, Scott suggests that the metaphor for grace in the parable is the call to go into the vineyard rather than the wages received. The parable's point is that entrance into the kingdom of God is by invitation rather than by merit; people are justified and accepted by God's gift and call to them, not by their work. That is also Paul's message when he writes to the Romans that, for all who believe, "there is no distinction, since all have sinned and fall short of the glory of God; they are now justified by his grace as a gift. . . . For we hold that a person is justified by faith apart from works prescribed by the law" (3:22-24, 28).

The lesson of the parables of the kingdom is that entrance into the kingdom is by gift and invitation, not by what we call law and order. Because of the social turmoil and lawlessness presently growing in the United States and other countries, more and more candidates running for public office are running on a law-and-order ticket. Law-and-order candidates want the order of law, and, for ease of presentation and clarity of political goals, such candidates tend to reduce justice and order to the execution of a measurable standard. For the protection of society, for ex-

3. Scott, *Hear Then the Parable*, p. 297.

ample, legislation such as "three times and you're out" is proposed: any offender who has been convicted of three violent felonies, with the last conviction by a federal court in the United States, is to be imprisoned for life with no possibility of parole or release. In such a view, justice, law, and order are equated with abstract categories. It is categories that are to be fulfilled, not personal relations. Three times and you're out; numerical categories rule.

Christians are admonished to live by the spirit of the law rather than the letter of the law. The reason is simple. A law, to be a law, is stated in universal form: a law is an objective statement of an action to be applied the same way at all times in all cases that fall under its jurisdiction. The spirit of the law is more than and different from the letter of the law because a person is more than and different from an object. Order brought to society by law is external order immediately visible; it is the order achievable among objects that can be grouped and placed together by categories. Order can be easily restored to a child's untidy playroom, for example, by putting all the blocks in one box and all the stuffed animals in another box. An evening curfew on city streets will visibly clear the streets of human traffic and any disorderly individuals after an appointed hour.

Treating people as objects is the quickest way to bring visible order to society. Regarding people who get in the way as no more than objects appears to lie at the base of the alarming growth of homicide rates in the United States. A young boy is killed for his leather jacket and athletic shoes, or a driver is shot for honking at another car on the street; sometimes an innocent person is slain simply because the perpetrator "just wanted to see what it would feel like to kill someone." The good order of our cities is clearly deteriorating with the growth of such behavior, and it is obvious that better order must be established. Many of the most vocal advocates of law and order believe that the universal establishment of capital punishment is the answer. A life for a life is objectively — and so obviously — just, it is said. A letter to the editor in the December 23, 1993, issue of the *Kansas City Star* put it this way:

> My question is this: Why do good people choose to let evil live?
>
> By not passing the death penalty we are breeding a society of murderers and monsters.
>
> Pass the death penalty and put an end to this madness.

The letter writer has no difficulty in objectively identifying good people and evil people. If good is opposed to evil, good people must oppose evil people. It clearly follows that, if good is to do away with evil, good people must do away with evil people. Killing those who are evil rather than letting them go on living and using up the resources of good people is the only way to avoid madness.

I would not offer as an illustration such a grotesque misunderstanding of personal nature and human complexity if it did not actually exist. To find such an absolute reduction of persons to objective, impersonal elements, however, strikingly reveals the latent presuppositions of other arguments that are more delicately put and that are more acceptable in appearance.

Limited time and limited resources circumscribe everything human beings undertake by themselves alone. Justice based on limited time and exhaustible resources is very different from mercy arising from unlimited time and infinite resources. The conflict between kingdoms — God's and ours — has a time-honored place in Christian theology. The point of the parables of the kingdom to which I have referred is that *the* kingdom is *God's,* not ours. Since God's kingdom is sustained by God's resources, life within it is very different from life within the kingdoms we make in the world. God's resources, based on abundance, produce very different results from our resources, based on scarcity.

In the human world, capital punishment as just punishment for murder is justified in the name of the victims who have been killed and in the name of protecting society. Is it unreasonable or too cynical to suggest that, because of our limited time and resources, such punishment is rather commended because we do not want to continue to relate to criminal offenders in the full complexity of their lives? It takes too much time and causes too much trouble; we have neither the time nor the patience to spend on such people.

We are a highly individualistic society, and thus we believe that the state is fulfilling its function when it protects us from foreign invasion, supplies basic services and empowerments, and protects us from each other as we live our individual lives with the greatest autonomy and freedom possible. Is it not possible that the desire to put murderers to death, in the name of the victims killed, is our society's way of "honorably" forgetting both the death of the victims and the problems of the killers as soon as possible, the quicker to get on with our own lives the way we want to? When a murderer is killed in the name of the victim, an equality is established between the two, and society can forget them both in the common bond of the death they share. Things are "right" again because a balance has been struck.

Persons are living subjects who, in their responsibility and free will, act differently from impersonal objects. Personal action is responsible action, responding appropriately on different occasions in different ways. We expect persons to make decisions that consider the future as well as the past; mechanical action, on the other hand, can only continue the past into the future, turning the future into the past. Truly personal action is not the same everywhere; mechanical action is. The machine we can depend on is the one that never lets us down; we can count on its behaving in the future just as it has in the past. When we slam on the brakes, we expect the car to stop immediately, not spurt forward. But pushing the brake is different from pushing the driver. If we push a driver too far, we cannot be sure what will happen.

Endless sameness is a way of describing the first law of motion: a physical body put in motion will remain indefinitely in that motion unless it is acted upon by external forces. Stability is a personal virtue. A characteristic of the people we call our friends is their dependability; we feel we can depend upon them for their support and encouragement whenever we call upon them and in whatever circumstances we may find ourselves. Nevertheless, people who act mechanically are not the ones we call our friends; they are not full persons. Their sameness is boring and stifling; it is something we flee.

When we see someone do a job perfunctorily, we say that the person isn't putting his or her heart into the task; we mean the action is performed routinely and so mechanically. Bureaucratic action is perfunctory action precisely because of its mechanical, impersonal nature. The bureaucratic action of government agencies is constantly criticized for being insensitive and unresponsive to human need; the most obvious goal of bureaucratic procedures seems to be the perpetuation and protection of the bureau and its employees through a slavish devotion to the book. Bureaucracy is the institutionalization of the letter of the law.

The truly human world is a responsive, sensitive world in which change and newness are not only possible but necessary. As human beings we are ourselves only in a world of change in which the future can be different from the past. The human world is also a social world in which we live with others. In that world, who can deny our need to live with each other in a truly personal, responsive, and creative manner? Personal action, as opposed to mechanical action, is action appropriate to the situation in which we find ourselves. We act differently with different people (we do not use the same vocabulary when talking to small children that we use when talking to adults), and we act differently with the same person at different times (we joke about someone's slip of the tongue but not about his falling down stairs).

If we are to be the full selves that we can be in the future, the consequences of our actions in the past must not be mechanically perpetuated. Fullness of personal living requires that from time to time we be able to turn new pages in our lives, or, as it is otherwise put, to turn a corner and take a new direction. To be fully ourselves, we need to be able to escape from the past — from the consequences of our past acts.

No one denies that in our lives together in the world we need a future both different from and better than the past. The search for something better is the basic motive of human effort and ambition. The world we make in our lives with each other needs to be changed; since that world is something we make in our relations with each other, if that world is to be changed, we must be changed. Our relations with each other must not be mechanical, merely repeating and perpetuating the past. What is sometimes called "honor" or "tradition" must be seen for what it really is: the mechanical, impersonal perpetuation of the past disguised by a name to make it sound personal and appropriate.

If we are not going to let our lives together be destroyed by impersonal, mechanical forces — if we need to make a complete break with our bondage to the past and escape impersonal enslavement — what is the most radical and different thing we can do? It is to forgive! Only forgiveness can change what is otherwise inevitable, for forgiveness is a free act that interrupts and changes, by the freedom of its bestowal, the internal necessity of mechanical inevitability.

An act of forgiveness is a free act that allows someone else to be free. Forgiveness, an act of mercy, is a gift one person makes to another; it is the infusion of something new into the life of another, enabling that person's life to become new from a source totally outside itself. To forgive is an act of mercy that cannot be required; it cannot be earned or deserved. No matter how small an act of mercy may appear, it is always a totally free act on the part of the person who bestows it and a totally new gift in the life of the person who receives it. It is a gift of a new beginning that is able to turn a person's life around completely. It is the gift of music to a paralyzed limb.

Human beings destroy each other and establish their kingdoms in the world by mechanically depersonalizing each other and defining justice in terms of abstract categories. God's world — God's kingdom — is different. Jesus does not come to us either to be or to deliver an abstract truth that we are left to apply to our lives as we are able. In Jesus, God comes to us on his own initiative, and for his own reasons, in the fullness of a person. God's mercy upon us and forgiveness of us in Jesus is not an abstract principle of mercy and forgiveness; it is God immediately entering the totality of our lives in the fullness of Jesus' life so that we can live Jesus' life as our life. Living in Christ, we live in the unlimited resources of God. When we accept God's gift of himself to us in Christ, we live with a totally different consciousness and see everything from a totally different perspective. *Everything* is different, not just a few things. We find ourselves actually doing what we could not even think of doing before. Forgiven, we can only forgive; living in God's mercy, we can only be merciful.

When we recognize ourselves in the presence of another, we feel ourselves held in focus by the other. When we know ourselves in the presence of Jesus, his strength already given to us allows us to see ourselves for the first time — in his eyes — for what we truly are. Only in the merciful presence of God do we know our sin for what it is. We can never first know our sin in its true nature and magnitude by ourselves and then come to God with it. When we know our sin for what it really is in Christ, we experience a love that only forgives, for it is a love that, in the end, has more power to accept us than we have to oppose it. In Christ, the creativity of love is more powerful in our lives than either the destructiveness of our sin or our denial of our sin. Neither our destructiveness nor our denial can overcome God's acceptance of us in Jesus. The sacrifice of Jesus for us is God's gift of himself to us — even if we try to destroy his gift on the cross.

God's unfailing creative love for us is shown in Jesus; that is why Jesus accepts us with an acceptance deeper than our being. Jesus accepts us in the deepest roots of our being, the roots lying beneath our consciousness, from which our conscious lives arise. Thus our acceptance by Jesus is even more than our consciousness of him; that is why we can trust our whole selves — conscious and unconscious, known and unknown — to him. That is why, in him, we experience a peace that passes understanding. It *is* in God that we live, move, and have our being.

6

The Intimacy of God's Word in Our Lives

EVERYTHING significantly Christian originates in the life of Jesus, and when I say "the life of Jesus" I mean not the story told about his life but the actual events of his life. The universe as a whole and our lives within the universe are a series of interacting events, and the fullness of the reality of the universe and of our lives in it is found only in the action of the events, not in our abstract thought about or our intellectual analysis of the events.

The life of Jesus is nothing less than the events and activities through which Jesus interacted with the events and activities of other people's lives. Because Jesus lived almost two thousand years ago, to say that everything significantly Christian originates in Jesus' life is to say that everything significantly Christian originated in past history. The unique thing about the Jesus of past history in Christian witness is that, although Jesus lived in the past, the events and activities of his life can be neither limited to the past nor reduced to the past. The life of Jesus is not what Christians claim it to be if the events of that life can be restricted to the past.

Jesus was recognized by his disciples to be the Messiah, the Christ, for whose coming the Jews were looking. The reason why the coming of the Messiah was looked for and anticipated was the belief that life would change and get better when the Messiah came. The messianic age would be a new age in which God's will ruled triumphantly; once the Messiah came, God's reign in the world would make a lasting change in the world. The coming would inaugurate God's lasting victory; it would not be a singular event that, in the passage of time, would be reduced to no more than a memory in a receding past.

While it is true that the life of Jesus — if Jesus is the Messiah — cannot be confined to the past, the reality of Jesus' life in the past is nevertheless most important. The Christian life is one of faith and trust in God, but that faith and trust are based on the reality of events that are claimed actually to have happened in the world. Faith and trust are acts of will, but Christian trust in God is not arbitrary trust, and Christian faith is not credulity. Christian faith and trust are reasonable faith and trust, and their reasonableness comes from the reality of the events from which they spring.

Christians, like everyone else, must live in the world, and, if their faith is to make a difference in their lives in the world, that faith must have the strength and the reality of the world. Because Christians believe that Jesus is the Word of God made flesh, they believe that God enters the events constituting their lives in the events constituting Jesus' life. In Jesus, God gives his love the reality of our world for us, and it is in the assurance of that reality that Christian faith makes its witness. The reality of something that has already happened in the world is the continuing source of Christians' trust of God in the events of their lives.

The meaning of the resurrection is that the event of Jesus' life — the action and activity of his life — continues in the moving present of today for what it was in Jesus' life on earth. The resurrection of Jesus and the gift of the Spirit mean that Jesus' life has not ended as an ongoing event in the world; they mean that Jesus is always newly coming to us offering the total dependence on God of his life to us. When we believe in the resurrection of Jesus, the difference that the event of Jesus' life made in the lives of his disciples is the very difference that he brings to our lives today. The difference that Jesus' life made in the lives of others was the reality that made his life an event in the world, and it is the continuing reality of that event in the world which makes the difference in the lives of Christians today.

Although Jesus' resurrection was an event in past history, the meaning of Jesus' resurrection cannot be separated from our lives. If Jesus is the Christ, the truth *of* Jesus cannot be limited *to* Jesus. Jesus is not just a human being. When Christians profess Jesus to be the Word of God made flesh, they recognize that Jesus is not just an individual who lived and died in the past but God intimately speaking to each one of us about himself or herself. Because Jesus is the Word of God made flesh, his life tells us about our lives; the life Jesus lives speaks to us about the possibilities of our existence. The resurrection of Jesus as the Christ means that the resurrection of Jesus is not a historic event that can be known for what it is only in the Jesus of past history; the resurrection of Jesus as the Christ means that the victory of *that* resurrection is offered to our lives now with the reality of Jesus' life in the world.

We cannot know Jesus as the Christ if we confine him to the past. On the other hand, we cannot know Jesus as the Christ if we confine him to the future, either. To say that Jesus now lives in heaven in a new state or condition different from ours isolates Jesus from us just as effectively as isolating him in the past; it removes his reality from us and from our world. Attempts to recall what we did not experience in the past or to anticipate something we have not yet experienced in the future are equally unhelpful.

If Jesus is isolated in either the past or the future, the reality of his life is reduced to talk. We all know the difference between saying and doing. What we say does not have the fullness of reality of what we do, and what is said about Jesus does not have *any* of the reality of his life. Jesus was recognized to be the Son of God because of the difference his life made in the lives of those who knew him; as I have been saying, the reality of his life showed in the change he made in the lives of those who became his disciples. Jesus' presence changed the way those who recognized him to be the Messiah lived in the world; Jesus' presence changed the way they were present in the world — and changed the way the world was present for them. All of that was what Paul meant when he said that in Christ we become a new creation.

Jesus' life changed the lives of his disciples because the activity of his life changed the activity of their lives. Jesus did not come to suggest a new way we might think about things. The incarnate Word of God came to change our lives, not just our thoughts. The world and our lives are chains of events in which we are caught up; neither the world nor our lives are strings of ideas by means of which we stand back from reality and comment on it instead of being caught up in it. I have commented on the temporal nature of our lives as persons and about how we can neither be persons nor know persons in an instant. Life is a process, and our basic perception of reality is a process. To live is to use time, and to live together is to use time together.

The life of Jesus centered a new way of living in the world; as I have been saying, Jesus did not come to suggest some new ideas about the world. One of the strange things about Jesus' life was that, although he brought a new way of living into the world during his lifetime, the full power of his life showed more fully in the lives of others after his death than during his life before his death. The record shows that Jesus' life became more effective — more itself in others — after his crucifixion and resurrection than before. The unique thing about the resurrection is that, after Jesus died, his life was not remembered for what it was; it was newly experienced for what it is. The historical record of the growth of the early church from a frightened and disappointed band of disciples in Jerusalem to a courageous and enthusiastic movement throughout the Roman Empire in just a few generations shows how the life of Jesus became newly effective after his death. It was not the memory of a dead Jesus but the presence of the living Jesus that activated the early church.

If Jesus is to live today in any significant sense for us, he must be able to enter and change our lives just as he entered and changed the lives of his first disciples after the resurrection. Although we are removed in time from the first disciples, we are not at as much of a disadvantage as it is sometimes supposed. It was the resurrected Jesus — the Jesus known after his death — who changed the disciples' lives, and it is the same Jesus who changes our lives. It was Jesus' presence with his followers after his resurrection that changed them from a handful of mourners to triumphantly free witnesses to new life in him. When we believe in the resurrection, the immediate presence of the living Jesus found in the lives of the first disciples is found in our lives also. The resurrection of Jesus means that the removal of Jesus from us in time has been as completely overcome as his removal from us by death. Jesus' resurrection is his victory over his burial in the past just as completely as it is his victory over his burial in the ground. The moving spirit of his life can still become the moving spirit of our lives because his spirit is the Spirit of God.

I have referred to Jesus' being present with us in the world today through his Spirit, his message, and the sacramental meal he instituted. All three modes of his presence can be talked about; such discussion is natural and necessary and is an important component of the life we share in Christ, but it also presents us with the constant danger of reducing the three dimensions of Jesus' presence to no more than words. Remembering that Jesus is the enfleshed Word of God is our safeguard against such reduction; there is only one Jesus, and the oneness of his person in each of the three modes of his presence means that each of the modes we can distinguish is its true self only with and in the other two. No one of the three can be isolated from the others, for none is a thing in itself. Each is a vehicle of the one person. The Spirit, the message, the sacrament of Jesus — each is a way that Jesus is present to us; each is a way that we experience his presence in our lives — a way that the events of his life enter the events of our lives.

When the reality of Jesus' life enters our lives, the reality of our lives is called into question. So put, God's entering our lives in Jesus sounds threatening — even frightening. The basic purport of the statement is that, in the Christian experience, reality speaks to reality.

The reality that speaks to reality in the presence of one person to another is shown in the difference one person's presence makes to another. Specific persons make specific differences in our lives. We relate differently to our mate, our parents, our employer, our children, our friends, and our enemies. The difference each makes to us is the presence of each to us; a person who makes no difference to us is not present to us. Every person in his or her self is a unique, singular subject, and if that person is truly present to me, he or she will make a unique, singular difference to me.

The specific difference a person makes in our lives is the key to the degree of presence that person has in our lives. Truly personal presence cannot be generalized, for there is no such thing as a general person. Every person is as specific as the time he or she lives.

God's Word become flesh means that God speaks to each of us as a specific person in the unique and specific situations in which we find ourselves. God's Word is not a general rule to be generally applied; it is a specific presence to each one of us in the specificity of each of our lives. In Jesus, God comes to us in the concrete situations in which we find ourselves. Our fleshly lives are our specific lives, and it is in those lives that the Word made flesh seeks us.

Our intimate lives are composed of the specific decisions we make for our own reasons in the changing circumstances of our lives. I have been saying that we know ourselves and that other persons know us in the way we use time, and the decisions we make in our lives are the ways we use the time of our lives. Personal intimacy requires the mutual sharing of time. When God's Word became flesh, God's Word became temporal, which means that, in Jesus, God comes to live time with us. To accept a person, we have seen, is to accept that person's use of time. Because we have all done things we later wish we had not, our tendency is to build our self-image out of some periods of our lives to the exclusion of others. In such a selective knowledge of ourselves, we do not acknowledge our whole selves. Denying we were ourselves when we did something that now embarrasses us is a way of denying ourselves. It is a temptation we all fall into as we try to sustain our fragile egos by ourselves.

The continuing scandal of Christianity is that, when the truth of ourselves is fully known, God accepts us more fully than we accept ourselves. God's acceptance of us in Jesus is a full acceptance free of all denial. In Jesus' crucifixion, God shows us that he loves us even when we do not love ourselves, for it is our truest selves that we try to kill on the cross. The mercy that God shows us in Jesus' giving himself to us is God's acceptance of us even in the totality of our rebellion against him. No matter what we do or have done, God never withdraws the offer of his love from us. Love is always given freely; it is never reactionary. God's never-failing, creative gift of love to us is the gift of his never-failing mercy and forgiveness. God's mercy and forgiveness are without measure or proportion. It is scandalous!

It is because God's mercy scandalizes us that we do not accept

[83]

it. Because we know we are unworthy of the limitless mercy that God offers us, our sense of justice makes us refuse it. We continue to stake out independent territory that is ours alone from which we can judge God. Once again we find that the problem is our judgment, not God's. Our total dependence upon God is too much for us to accept. God's difference from us is found in the fact that there is nothing God cannot accept, for there is nothing from which God must defend himself.

Living with Jesus in the minute-by-minute flow of our lives, we are not with him only on occasion. We cannot present the events of our lives to God in Christ for the first time after the events are over and then ask God for a summary judgment of them. The enfleshed Word of God, Jesus, after his resurrection, lives in and through time with us in our fleshly lives. Jesus' moving presence with us in time is a resource we are never without; that is why Jesus' presence with us is an intimate presence. The intimate presence of Jesus is the temporal presence of Jesus. That is how Jesus is with us "all the days," as the literal translation of the Greek usually translated "always" reads (see Matt. 28:20).

God's mercy and acceptance are gifts that God continually offers us before we ask for them (cf. 1 John 4:19). I have suggested that it is impossible for us to know our sins fully by ourselves in order to bring them to God for mercy; we can fully recognize our sin and denial of God only by first being in — and being strengthened by — God's loving presence. We can recognize our sin only in God's mercy, not in order to obtain God's mercy. More scandal!

The Jesus Prayer illustrates our quandary. A short variation of the prayer is "Lord Jesus Christ, Son of God, have mercy on me, a sinner"; an even shorter version is "Lord Jesus, have mercy on me, a sinner." This prayer, as is well known, is said in synchronization with one's breathing. Many people are put off by it because it appears to be totally self-centered at its best and self-condemnatory at its worst. There are people who use the prayer but omit the phrase "on me, a sinner." It is too much for them continually to present themselves to God through Christ as sinners. Sin is what they want to put behind them and get away from, and a more positive, affirmative relation with God is what they want to develop.

The problem with omitting the phrase "on me, a sinner" from the Jesus Prayer is that the joy and intimacy of God's love for us in Jesus are then lost. If I drop this phrase from the prayer, I also remove the specificity of my life from it. I substitute a general desire for the future for the actual decisions I have made and the actual life I have lived in the past. Instead of accepting the mercy of God's forgiveness of what I have actually done — and so letting God into the only reality my life has — I want to substitute a new life with God in the future that forgets my life in the past. But such a life with God would not be my true life, for I am and always will be my past as well as my present and my future. God does not save me by denying a part of me; God does not save any of us by denying a part of us.

Forgiving is not forgetting. Our past is part of our identity; we are not ourselves without it. Forgiveness does not forget the past; rather, forgiveness relegates the past to the past so that it can no longer limit the present and compromise the future. By accepting but confining the past to the past, forgiveness liberates us in the wholeness of our being to accept the new life that the resurrected and glorified Christ offers us out of our future.

To say that the risen Jesus died to death means that, in the resurrection, death was so confined to the past that it can no longer be a threat to the future. That is what forgiveness does to sin; forgiveness removes the obstacles we have placed between God and us in the past so that we can fully receive God's ongoing gift of himself to us in the future.

When we pray "Lord Jesus, have mercy on me, a sinner," we

are saying something that can be said only in Jesus' presence. The Jesus Prayer is not a means of achieving Jesus' presence. It is not a way of asking for Jesus' presence; it is the acknowledgment of the "operation" of his presence already with us. I have said repeatedly, as the First Letter of John says, that Jesus comes to us, is present with us, and offers his mercy to us before we either search for him or ask him to come to us. We can accept his presence, but we cannot produce it. His coming to us before we can ask him to come is our reassurance and our joy! There is nowhere we can be without his help, for he does not wait for us to call for help.

Joy that Jesus' mercy is ours before we ask for it is what Jesus turns our sorrow for our sin into, as his active presence permeates the active presence of our lives. Joy arising from the gratuity of God's mercy in Jesus is our liberation from the past and the energizing source of our not sinning in the future. In the unfailing security of God's mercy, we are liberated to do what we want to do — to celebrate the freedom his mercy gives us by accepting all of it and living it with others. When we live our liberation and freedom in Christ, we find ourselves actually doing things we could not even think of doing before.

That is the dynamism of Christian living. When I am living minute by minute with Jesus, he is intimately present in my life. When I acknowledge my freely willed separation from him in the past, when I did not want to be with him, I acknowledge my separation from God and the results of such separation that accumulate in the anxiety of my life. When I acknowledge what my life is and has been when I live it by myself for myself, I acknowledge that I am in fact a sinner, because I am my past, and my past cannot be denied. In the presence of Jesus, my only comfort comes from acknowledging my sin, not trying to deny it. The comfort rather than the discomfort of such acknowledgment comes from the presence of Jesus overcoming my presence to myself independently of him.

We acknowledge our total dependence on Jesus by acknowledging the sinfulness of our activity — the separation of our lives from him — when we put ourselves in the place of God. Acknowledging ourselves to be sinners to the extent that we replace God with ourselves is the way we acknowledge our total dependence upon God as his creatures. Once we fully accept and live the total dependence upon God that we are in our finite, threatened being, we are able to live the structure and joy of the Jesus Prayer without having to use any of its words. Then this prayer, first known as the prayer of breathing, truly becomes the prayer of the heart. Then our life is God's life, and our joy and liberation are complete. When we fully let God into our lives, his presence flows through us to others. Obstructions in our lives disappear. When we live the Jesus Prayer, its structure, which at first seemed self-centered, actually releases us from ourselves for the service of others. The only mercy is God's mercy, and once we experience and live that mercy there are no bounds to it in our lives. Questions of justice or concern for ourselves never keep us from loving others.

7

From a Full Understanding to a New Understanding

GOD'S WORD always speaks to us in the specific situations of our lives. The only world in which we live our fully personal lives is the world at hand; that is the world God entered in Jesus, and it is in that world that Jesus comes to us and remains with us today.

Think of the difference Jesus would make in our lives if we knew and accepted him really living in the world in which we live. The immediate world of our lives is a world of decision: we are so immediately in that world that everything in it is a decision or amounts to a decision. In the abstract world of our thought, we contemplate possibilities and muse about choices, but in the immediate world of our fleshly lives everything we do has an either/or aspect. Either we do this or we do that: either we sit or we stand; either we delay or we act; either we keep our eyes open or we close them; either we go or we stay; either we are honest or we are dishonest; either we pay attention or we let our minds wander.

Life in the flesh is a specific life; it is not an abstract entity equally shared by all. My fleshly life is mine alone; no one lives it but me. The Word made flesh speaks to me in that life, in the

[89]

life that is no one else's but mine. God's Word never addresses any of us in a general way, treating us as no more than one instance of a common nature. In Jesus, the Word of God made flesh speaks to us in our flesh. There is no way to generalize the contact. That is what the author of the letter to the Hebrews was saying, in his manner, when he wrote, "Indeed, the word of God is living and active, sharper than any two-edged sword, piercing until it divides soul from spirit, joints from marrow; it is able to judge the thoughts and intentions of the heart. And before him no creature is hidden, but all are naked and laid bare to the eyes of the one to whom we must render an account" (4:12-13).

The immediacy and the specificity of our lives in the flesh are most convincingly shown by the immediacy and specificity of our death. The axiom of the existentialists is that everyone dies his or her own death. Death comes to each one of us as his or her death alone; no one else can die for us.

It is commonly noted that, in the four Gospels, the accounts of the passion and death of Jesus are given a disproportionate amount of space and treatment when compared with the accounts given the rest of his life. There is a simple explanation for this disparity. The death of Jesus was of overwhelming importance to the first disciples and to the early church, for it was the reality of Jesus' death that testified to the reality of his life. Jesus' death was important, but it was the *reality* of the death that was the primary concern. The reality of death, as I have just indicated, is the ultimate reality for which there is no substitute, and it is with a reality that cannot be substituted for that God enters the un-substitutable reality of each of our lives. The Good News brought by Jesus is that the reality of his death is the key to the reality of his resurrection; that makes the reality of his death the key to the reality of his victory over death in our lives.

The key role played by the reality of Jesus' death for the first Christians is also the key to understanding the selection of the documents that eventually made up the canon of the New Testament, according to William Farmer. He suggests that the striking similarity of the four canonical Gospels, when compared with other gospel literature, is "their consistent emphasis upon the flesh and blood existence, passion, and martyrdom of Jesus Christ as Son of God. . . . All other extant gospel literature failed to feature the flesh and blood martyrdom of Jesus."[1] Farmer goes on to discuss the Diocletian persecution of the church in the early fourth century in Gaul, when the emperor ordered all copies of scripture to be handed over and destroyed. During the persecution, Christian worship was prohibited and Christian churches were demolished. Christians had no recourse to law; all clergy were ordered arrested, and they could obtain their release only after offering sacrifice to the emperor. The surrender of scripture played a crucial role; those who kept scripture were sought out and hunted down. To hand over scripture amounted to apostasy in the eyes of the church, but to keep scripture amounted to a death sentence in the state. In these circumstances the significance of a book of scripture was determined by whether or not it was a book worth dying for. In Farmer's view, the answer to the question became a decisive element in the selection of the books in the canonical New Testament. For early Christians during their persecution, the message of scripture was not just words; it directly affected their lives in the flesh! The teaching of scripture was not abstracted from Jesus' life and death.

The account of Jesus' passion and death is one of the few components found in all four Gospels. Jesus' eating a meal with his disciples, a meal that took place just before his betrayal and death and that was associated with the Passover, is also mentioned in all four Gospels. In Luke and in Paul's First Letter to the

---

1. Farmer, *Jesus and the Gospel: Tradition, Scripture, and Canon* (Philadelphia: Fortress Press, 1982), p. 161.

Corinthians, the meal, known as the Last Supper, is taken to be the institution of the eucharist because of Jesus' telling the disciples to "do this in remembrance of me" (Luke 22:19; 1 Cor. 11:23-25). The Gospel of John gives no institutional force to the meal, but the Gospel mentions the supper Jesus had with his disciples at the time (John 13:1-2), and the common consensus is that Jesus' "bread of life" discourse, recounted in the sixth chapter of the Gospel (to which we will shortly turn), makes sense only as a commentary on the significance of the eucharist.

In the universal life of the church, the ritual meal that Jesus shared with his disciples just before the Passover has always had a unique relation with — to the point of identity with — the life of Jesus verified by the reality of his death. That was the reason Paul said, "For as often as you eat this bread and drink the cup, you proclaim the Lord's death until he comes" (1 Cor. 11:26). A few verses earlier, Paul stated that he received from the Lord what he had handed on — "that the Lord Jesus on the night when he was betrayed took a loaf of bread, and when he had given thanks, he broke it and said, 'This is my body that is for you. Do this in remembrance of me.' In the same way he took the cup also, after supper, saying, 'This cup is the new covenant in my blood. Do this, as often as you drink it, in remembrance of me'" (vv. 23-25). The meaning of the Greek that is translated "in remembrance of me" is "to recall me" or "to make me present." What is done in the eucharist in remembrance of Jesus, then, is actually the recalling and making present of the living Jesus. The remembrance is not *about* Jesus' life; it *is* his life.

We must not be put off by Paul's statement that, in the eucharist, we proclaim the Lord's death. The eucharist is an exercise in living, not dying. There is no dead Christ. The living Christ once died, but the only Christ we can recall is the one now living in glory. The death proclaimed in the eucharist, as we saw, is the reality of the living, resurrected Jesus. The point is that it is precisely the Jesus who died who is the living one now with us. The story of the appearance of the resurrected Jesus to the two disciples on their way to Emmaus is significant here. As the two disciples were talking about the events that had recently happened, Jesus, unrecognized, joined them and asked what they were talking about. The disciples told him about the betrayal and death of the one they followed and about the empty tomb. Toward evening, the disciples asked Jesus to stay with them, and, in the course of the evening meal, Jesus "took bread, blessed and broke it, and gave it to them. Then their eyes were opened, and they recognized him; and he vanished from their sight" (Luke 24:30-31). After Jesus left them, "they said to each other, 'Were not our hearts burning within us while he was talking to us on the road, while he was opening the scriptures to us?' " (v. 32). The disciples recognized Jesus during the meal: the living Jesus was with them as the three of them shared time together doing something together. As they walked, talked, and ate, the chain of events of Jesus' life intersected and penetrated the chain of events of the disciples' lives.

In the eucharist we meet, and are meant to recognize, the living Jesus. Jesus initiated, instituted, and personally willed the meal in which we participate. In so willing the eucharist for us, Jesus comes to us in the ongoing action of his life; the Spirit and message of Jesus are in the meal because Jesus willed the meal to be the active presence of his life and message. Every meal in which Jesus participated was given special significance by his presence. Through the way Jesus lived in the world, we have seen, the world was re-created in his Spirit, the Spirit of God. In the eucharist Jesus instituted, Jesus gathered up and made available to us — that is, he newly created — a means by which the action of his life enters the action of our lives, so that his re-creation of the world could continue in our lives. Jesus' freely willed action made available to us in the Last Supper is the one thing Jesus told his disciples to do: "Do this," he said "to recall me." Our wills are in special alignment with Jesus' will — indeed, his will becomes our will — when we accept his gift of himself to us in the eucharistic action.

Powerful words are now beginning to roll. Important consequences are beginning to unfold from rather simple-sounding premises. Before we proceed and get carried away, perhaps it would be wise to pause a moment or two for a reality check. After almost two thousand years of eucharistic celebration, we may ask how immediately Jesus is known and recognized in the eucharist. How intimately is the life of Jesus found in the lives of those who receive the sacramental food of his body and blood? How many people feel they truly share Jesus' life in the ritual meal in which they participate? We say that the eucharist was instituted at the "Lord's Supper," but we may ask whether or not it really is the Lord's Supper — Jesus' meal — we go to when we go to the eucharist. Liturgical scholars wax eloquent about the significance of meals and of eating together in antiquity, but this is the fast-food era. We don't have time to eat together; we don't even have time to sit down and eat by ourselves. We eat on the go, in the car, on the run. We order meals instead of allowing our meals to order us. Today, family members scatter when they eat — they carry their meals to their rooms, to their television sets, to their computers, or wherever the activities they do not want interrupted are located.

In our churches, how often is the eucharist thought of as just a service we or someone else puts on? Such services tend to be known primarily by the words used in them, words in a book or a church bulletin we hold before our eyes, words that have become familiar to our ears through years of repetition. To be sure, ritual actions are going on during the service, but the actions or events that catch our attention are more apt to be distractions than aids to our understanding; when that is the case, the only real continuity of the service is the static order of the words. Our tendency to reduce ritual meaning to words is illustrated by the clamor and distress caused in the last half of the twentieth century by liturgical renewal in the churches. If liturgical worship is reduced to words, then when the words are changed, everything is lost! That is precisely the loss which many people experienced in liturgical renewal, even though the changes commended to them were said by the experts to be "enrichments." For many, the worship of the church over the years has been reduced to static words rather than dynamic action.

Institutional order can be best kept and most easily taught if God's message to us in Jesus is reduced to verbal teaching. If we reduce something to words, we can objectively examine it and draw reasonable conclusions from it. If we can reduce God's message and presence with us to words, we can the more easily draw our conclusions from, and base our plans on, God's authority. If we can put God's message before us in propositional form, we can the more easily judge others by it. If God's revelation can be reduced to words, God's word judges us only by making verbal demands upon us, and verbal demands are objective demands. They are limited and precise. We can know with certainty when we have fulfilled our obligations. I'm sure I don't have to continue to develop the point, for we have obviously arrived again at a religion of law.

Now is the time for us to consider the sixth chapter of John's Gospel, which, although it does not overtly recount Jesus' words during the Last Supper, is overwhelmingly acknowledged to be a commentary on the eucharist. As the chapter begins, Jesus has gone up a mountain with his disciples, and we are told that the feast of the Passover is near. Sitting with his disciples, Jesus sees a large crowd coming toward him, and he asks Philip how they are going to buy enough bread for the multitude to eat. When Jesus is told that a boy has five barley loaves (thought to be the bread of the earliest eucharists) and two fishes, Jesus has the people sit down, and the story continues with the miraculous feeding of the five thousand. After the meal is over, the crowd wants forcibly to make Jesus king, but Jesus escapes and returns to the mountain by himself. That those in the crowd wanted to proclaim Jesus king shows their lack of discernment about what was really going on. The best that can be said for them is that they saw Jesus as the fulfillment of their old nationalistic expectations: they saw him as the potential leader of a triumphant political kingdom. But Jesus had not come to play that role in their lives. Consequently, he hid himself from them.

In the rest of the sixth chapter, Jesus crosses the sea to Capernaum and leads those he encounters from a total misunderstanding of who he is and what he has come for, through a full understanding of what can be known about him on the basis of Israel's past history, to a new understanding of him that cannot be attained by the past or future expectations of the people themselves. During this explanation, Jesus describes himself as the proper fulfillment of past expectation. Jesus does so because it is necessary for people to see him as the fulfillment of their previous hope and longing, to accept him at that level, so that he can lead them beyond themselves to God's unexpected gift of new life in him.

Jesus offers himself as the fulfillment of the expectation that people had before his coming by calling himself the bread of life who has come down from heaven to do the will of the one who sent him (vv. 35-38). As the people begin to complain and argue among themselves about how Jesus could be the bread from heaven, since they know him to be the son of Joseph and Mary, Jesus goes on to identify himself with the manna the Israelites ate in the wilderness after their escape from Egypt. Raymond E. Brown sees the bread to which Jesus compares himself in the phrase "bread of life" to be the teaching of the Torah, the Law.

The Old Testament source of Jesus' reference is found in Deuteronomy, where we read: "He humbled you by letting you hunger, then by feeding you with manna . . . in order to make you understand that one does not live by bread alone, but by every word that comes from the mouth of the LORD" (8:3). The Lord God is a God of hearing. He is the God who says, "Hear, O Israel: The LORD is our God, the LORD alone," and "Hear, O Israel, the statutes and ordinances that I am addressing to you today" (Deut. 6:4; 5:1).

The Torah that ancient Israel heard God speak to them was something to do. Once the Law was delivered, it was something to live by; it was a rule of life. The difficulty was that it tended to become a life of the letter of the Law rather than of the spirit. It was a life people lived under God for God.

For how many today, we may wonder, is religion primarily something heard? Religion is a synonym for "listening to lessons." People no longer speak of going to "hear mass," but although the phrase is no longer used, the practice is not necessarily past. In one way or another, the verbalization of religion seems to characterize its nature in the lives of many people. Hearing and thinking, with perhaps some meditation thrown into the mix, are the bases of our religious lives. Once we have so recognized and assimilated religious truths, it is our responsibility to try to practice them, as best we can, in our lives in the world.

Turning thought into action is not an easy task, as anyone knows who serves the general public and who resolves — before going to work — to be patient with demanding customers during the course of the coming day. Just walking down a crowded street with people dashing here and there, let alone trying to respond to people's specific demands and expectations, is enough to destroy a resolution of patience on the way to work.

Hearing what to do is not enough. We need more help than that — and, if we continue along in the sixth chapter of John's

Gospel, we will be offered more help. In verses 51-58 of the chapter, Raymond Brown discerns a new eucharistic theme dominating the discussion: "No longer are we told that eternal life is the result of believing in Jesus; it comes from feeding on his flesh and drinking his blood (54). . . . Even though the verses in 51-58 are remarkably like those of 35-50, a new vocabulary runs through them: 'eat,' 'feed,' 'drink,' 'flesh,' 'blood.'"[2]

The new truth to which Jesus now leads his listeners is that they (we) can have right *belief* only by *doing* something. They (we) must eat his flesh and drink his blood. Jesus says that the bread that he will give for the life of the world is his flesh. Upon hearing this, the people "disputed among themselves, saying, 'How can this man give us his flesh to eat?'" (vv. 51-52). The question is ours also.

The answer to the question of how Jesus can give us his flesh to eat is indicated in the preface to John's Gospel, where we read, "And the Word became flesh and lived among us" (1:14). As the word "flesh" is used in the passage, it is a synonym for Jesus' having "lived among us." The flesh we receive in the eucharist *is* Jesus' life in the world. In biblical usage, "flesh" refers not so much to *what* lives as to *how* a person lives. In our use of the terms, "body" is an abstract noun indicating a common feature of human existence; "flesh," on the other hand, has a concrete, singular meaning for us. We use the term "body" collectively to refer to a body (group) of people, but we never speak of a "flesh of people."

In biblical usage, "body" almost always had the same concrete meaning as "flesh," but, because of the change of connotation I have just noted, we miss the very essence of what Jesus was saying if we use the word "body" instead of "flesh" to describe Jesus'

2. Raymond E. Brown, S.S., *The Gospel according to John, 1-12*, Anchor Bible (Garden City, N.Y.: Doubleday, 1966), p. 284.

presence in the eucharist. I have read theological explications of the eucharist that commended the use of "body" instead of "flesh" precisely because of the abstract, common nature of the former. By this time it will come as no surprise to learn that I believe such usage completely misses the gift that the eucharist was instituted to offer us. The first Christians caused a scandal in the pagan world when it was rumored that, in their secret worship, they were cannibals eating someone's flesh; this is the scandal that Christians should cause in the unbelieving world of today — although not because of the charge of cannibalism. The scandal should be caused by the upheaval of secular values seen in the lives of those living by the resources of God in Christ.

"Flesh" carries a connotation of complexion, texture, intimacy, and immediacy; "body" does not. When people talk about their "bloodline," they are talking about the historical line of their flesh. To recognize one's bloodline is to recognize a singular history of shared time and identity through generations. Even though we meet someone for the first time, if that person is an aunt or an uncle or a cousin in our bloodline, we meet him or her with a feeling of intimacy that we do not normally feel when meeting a stranger. When we have a flesh-and-blood relation with someone else, we feel we have an interior relation in our lives with that person; we feel that a blood relation is somehow part of our condition. When Jacob's father Isaac told him not to marry a Canaanite woman, Jacob journeyed to the house of Laban, his mother's brother. When Laban, who had never seen Jacob before, learned that Jacob had come and who he was, he ran out to meet him, kissed and embraced him, and said, "Surely you are my bone and my flesh!" (Gen. 29:14). The two men established an immediate intimacy, and Jacob stayed with Laban, serving him for seven years before marrying Rachel.

The moving force of flesh-and-blood relations, when compared with the passivity of abstract concepts and principles, can be illustrated from world history near the end of the twentieth century as well as from Old Testament stories. A case in point is offered by Pope John Paul II's Christmas message of 1991. Referring to the fighting then going on in Yugoslavia and the suffering caused by the warring factions in Croatia, the pope called for an end to hatred and oppression in which "passions and violence are defying reason and common sense."

Even though the conflict defied reason and common sense, did knowledge of that fact move people to change their behavior? That the creating God gave all the participants in the conflict the same human nature appeared to be a meaningless and gratuitous irrelevance when judged by the hostile actions of those who shared that nature. Christians still fought Christians — as well as Muslims.

In the post–World War II era of the cold war, Yugoslavia, under Marshall Tito, appeared to be among the most prosperous and well-ordered satellite countries of the Soviet Union. However, during the war, the Croat government had collaborated with the Nazis in killing hundreds of thousands of Serbs, and some Bosnian Muslims had also cooperated in the extermination and deportation of Serbs. When Tito came to power, he imposed functional cooperation between the three ethnic communities, and he prohibited public discussion of the World War II experience. But in the fleshly lives of the people, internal communal identity and external communal hatred were undiminished throughout the years that Yugoslavia appeared to be one of the "best" satellite countries, and, when there was no longer sufficient external force to control the interrelations of the communities, the Serbs tried to capture as much land and power as they could to establish a new Serbian state.

The Serbians instituted the much-denounced policy of "ethnic cleansing," in the course of which the most heinous acts occurred: Serb soldiers set up rape camps for young women and girls; men were summarily rounded up and shot; a Croat child watched soldiers slice open a pregnant woman and remove her baby; Muslims were tortured and beaten to death. When asked how such things could be done to people, one Serb answered, "They are not people." Communal membership based on bloodlines and relations of the flesh did indeed move people to action. Communal identity of the flesh determined what would be done and what would be allowed. Christian principles, on the other hand, have been shown to make no difference at all in the conflict. Isn't the reason for such impotence the fact that Christianity cannot be reduced to principles or abstract concepts in the first place? The only truly Christian Word is the Word made flesh. That is where the action is; that is where our lives are lived; and that is where the Word of God is found!

I have said innumerable times that the life of the flesh is life in one's immediate situation in the world. Life in the flesh is good, and the fullness of that goodness is found in the life of Jesus. The life *of* the flesh, in contrast to life *in* the flesh, is repeatedly condemned in the New Testament, especially in the writings of Paul (see, among others, Gal. 5:16, 19; Eph. 2:3; Col. 2:23; 2 Pet. 2:18; 1 John 2:16). A careful reading will show that where the life of the flesh is condemned, it is the *lust* of the flesh that is usually referred to.

Our fleshly lives are our immediate lives; the lust of the flesh consists in emphasizing the immediacy of life in the present to the exclusion of the fullness of our lives, which extends beyond the present into the past and the future. The lust of the flesh is the immediate gratification of the flesh. When we live lustful lives, we seek our full meaning as persons in the changing immediacy of the world. In the lust of the flesh, we find our identity and security in the changing and transitory instead of in the stable and enduring. In the life (lust) of the flesh, we stake our personal identity on what does not last, thus reducing our lives to the level of things and possessions. As it is often said, when we live our lives this way, "having" is more important than "being." The possessions and experiences I have in the present are substituted for my truly personal being.

The life "of the flesh," in spite of its immediacy, is really an abstract life in which it is impossible for a person to be his or her full self, because it abstracts from the past and future every person as truly is as he or she is his or her present. In the immediacy of the fleshly life of Jesus, the past failures of our fleshly lives are forgiven, and the present of our fleshly lives is enriched out of a future that has no end. We will now move on to consider in more depth how God gives such a life to us.

8

Given a Life to Live

I HAVE SAID that the question "How can this man give us his flesh to eat?" is our question as well the question of those who first heard the words. When we understand the biblical use of the word "flesh," the question we and Jesus' first listeners ask is, "How can Jesus give us his life to live?" The truth of the matter is that Jesus meant nothing less by his words.

Jesus' words were " 'Very truly, I tell you, unless you eat the flesh of the Son of Man and drink his blood, you have no life in you. Those who eat my flesh and drink my blood have eternal life, and I will raise them up on the last day; for my flesh is true food and my blood is true drink'" (John 6:53-55). Commentaries stress that the Greek word translated "eat" means "to chew or gnaw"; the point is that both the reality of the eating and the reality of what is being eaten are highlighted. The verb is not metaphorical, not a reference to chewing something over in one's mind. When Jesus says that his flesh and blood are true food and true drink, he is stating not only that the food and drink are real food and drink, but also that those who eat and drink are really (truly) eating and drinking his life in the world. In Jesus' remark that those who eat his flesh and drink his blood have eternal life, we are being told, as Raymond Brown points out, that eternal life is the result not just of believing but of eating and drinking (i.e., actively accepting in our lives) the lived action of Jesus' life.

That the simple acts of eating and drinking could have such magnified significance furnishes a reason for Christianity's being considered either inconsequential or, once again, scandalous. On the one hand, the commonness of eating and drinking could lead one to believe there is nothing unusual in the eucharistic exercise of those activities; eating and drinking at the eucharist would then be said to be no different from eating or drinking anywhere. On the other hand, the spectacular scandal claimed for the eucharist is that the unique, singular life of the Son of God is made available to us and shared with us in such commonplace activities.

What is more common and usual than eating and drinking? Obviously, the specialness of eating and drinking at the eucharist is not found in the acts themselves; it is found in the use Jesus made of them. The actions are special because of Jesus' presence in them. Indeed, Jesus' eucharistic presence with us is the paradigm for his presence with us in all the activities of our lives. Our spiritual lives are not different from our regular lives. We have only one life, and in that life Jesus does not make part of it "spiritual" by calling us to be with him in a manner that removes us from the world. In our truly spiritual lives, we discover Jesus in the "usual," and we live with him in the common, mundane activities of the day. When we truly live with Jesus, he fills the ordinary with the intimacy of his presence, rather than calling us away from the common and ordinary in order to be with him. When we live in the Spirit of Jesus, Jesus' presence becomes a dimension of all life rather than being something known only in an isolated moment in a highly restricted manner under special circumstances.

Jesus consecrates the ordinary by his presence in it; thus he frees us amid everything in the world rather than enclosing us in a restricted portion of the world. The lesson of life in Christ is that, in a most important sense, there is nothing special about our religious life at all. We are to be religious everywhere and always; what is special about religion is found in the activity of our living — not in the place we may be at the moment. The religious life cannot be limited to activities going on in church buildings.

The newness of the situation created by Jesus' eucharistic gift of himself to others is emphasized as Jesus continues: "Just as the living Father sent me, and I live because of the Father, so whoever eats me will live because of me. This is the bread that came down from heaven, not like that which your ancestors ate, and they died. But the one who eats this bread will live forever" (John 6:57-58). As we have seen, the bread eaten in the wilderness was identified with the verbal teaching of God; but the new bread offered by Jesus is nothing less than Jesus' flesh and life, which is why those who eat this bread will live forever. The new bread from heaven is not just a new teaching; the only thing that truly lasts forever is Jesus' life as proven by the resurrection.

"Teaching" exists only in the mind of a living person. "Teaching" requires a person to teach it; it has no ability to exist or make a difference in anyone's life by itself. Words are just words, and what is said about words can be said about truth. "Truth," philosophically considered, is said to be either a consistent coherence of ideas among themselves or a certain correspondence between our ideas and a reality beyond them. In either alternative, truth in itself is inert, lifeless, and powerless. It does nothing; it achieves nothing. It is an abstract relationship, either among ideas or between ideas and things.

Truth is something to be achieved. The quest for truth is a personal quest requiring an individual to be truth's seeker and discoverer. Put in different words, truth does not exist in itself; it dwells in and qualifies something beyond itself. Its reality comes from the reality of the subjects who discover it and from the reality of the objects in which it is found.

We should now be able to see why the truth we find in knowledge, when we say that knowledge or a certain idea is true, cannot nourish life. Only life can nourish life; ideas do not give life, for in themselves they are inert and inanimate. Ideas — even true ideas — do nothing. We can freeze to death while thinking of fire, and we get no real help in our lives from God by merely thinking about God. When Jesus says that he *is* the truth (John 14:6), he means that the only lasting truth is the truth identified with his life. Life alone lasts and makes a difference; truth lasts only as an aspect of life. The only everlasting truth is everlasting life — the resurrected life — not ideas about that life.

We now have a new perspective from which to understand why Christian living does not proceed from thought to action. Abstract thought does nothing and moves no one. Ideas do not animate an injured leg. Action begins with action, and living begins with living.

The Christian life begins with Christian living, not with words about such living. Words and vocabulary systems always first arise within, only later to be abstracted from, activities and events that precede them. Children learn the language of their homes and communities by learning the names of the activities into which they are incorporated from birth onward. When they eat, children learn the words "to eat" and the nouns that refer to their favorite foods, and through their play children learn the words for running, stopping, standing, throwing, hiding — as well as prepositions such as "to," "by," "on," "under," and the nouns that refer to animals, toys, and friends.

Once we are oriented in the world through our bodies and the immediacy of our experience, we are able to construct abstract vocabulary systems and produce coherent ideational systems that are far more complex than anything we can experience through sensory perception. But all of those systems are ultimately rooted in the spatial and temporal orientation of our fleshly lives and the activities of those lives that began before intelligible speech. Christianity, too, has produced a number of abstract theological systems and propositions, but everything significantly true and effective in it originates in the lived activity of Jesus' enfleshed life and our participation in that life.

I have stressed the temporal nature of human life in our discussion, and the reported words of Jesus that we have just been considering refer to a temporal structure that corresponds precisely to the structure of our being. It is important to notice how Jesus' statement that "those who eat my flesh and drink my blood have eternal life, and I will raise them up on the last day" (John 6:54) folds into our ongoing lives. Jesus says that those who eat and drink his flesh and blood *have* eternal life in the present and that he *will* raise them up in the future. The message given to us is that those who will open their lives to Jesus' life by eating his flesh and drinking his blood will receive something in their lives now that will be consummated later. Jesus is the eschatological person; he is the Alpha and the Omega, the first and the last, the presence of the one "who is and who was and who is to come" (Rev. 1:8; 21:6; 22:13). The present and the future of our lives meet in Jesus, but also our spiritual past — for he is the bread the Israelites ate in the wilderness as well as the gift of our new future in the present.

Both the dynamism and the security of our lives in Christ arise from Jesus' words that "those who eat my flesh and drink my blood abide in me, and I in them" (John 6:56). The mutual indwelling of Jesus with those who eat his flesh and drink his blood, described by the verb "abiding" or "remaining," is the sharing of an ongoing activity that never ends. The permanence conveyed by the words "abiding" and "remaining" must not be confused with rest, passivity, and inactivity. Love is an action, and the God who is Love is an acting God. That is why everything Christian begins with and is located within the action of love.

Because our remaining in Jesus and his remaining in us is the permanence of an active, ongoing interpersonal relationship, nothing in our lives in Christ can be specified and known ahead of time. Everything is living, new, and exciting. As I have been saying, nothing fully Christian can be deduced or objectified; nothing follows from static premises. Everything grows out of the spontaneous presence of persons to each other. Our lives in Christ are dynamic, personal, all-consuming relationships.

Because of the dynamic, active nature of the Christian life, the clarification and direction of life in Christ grow out of a process of personal encounter with Jesus in time. That is why Christian clarification and direction are found in prayer, an activity of personal engagement, rather than in the delivery of sacred objects. The objective deliverance of guidance is found in the realm of law, but, when law rules supreme, its supremacy is always shown by killing life in the end. The spirit gives life; words without the spirit are dead and can produce nothing more than themselves.

In the light of what I have been saying, we can understand why prayer cannot be reduced to a form of words or to a special technique whose purpose is to produce a special relation with God. Nowhere is that truth more clearly seen than in the eucharist, where Jesus calls us to himself and gives himself to us on his own initiative. Any attempt to use prayer as a special means to produce a special effect — mystical experience, for example — is doomed to failure. True prayer, like true religion for a Christian, is the living of one's whole life in the Spirit of Jesus, thus being with God in all things and seeing God in all things. Neither prayer nor religion is a technique that produces God for us.

In our lighthearted moments we sometimes say that our whole lives are our prayer, but what we may intend as a joke in conversation is no joke in fact. If our lives and our prayer can be separated, neither our lives nor our prayer is Christian. We are to live with the one God in all that we do. God in Jesus is not closer to us one moment than another; in the resurrected Jesus, God is present with us moment by moment throughout our lives. The constant intimacy of God's presence in our lives in Jesus is the source of joy in all circumstances. "Eucharist" means "thanks-giving," and in the joy of Jesus' presence we live eucharistically, giving thanks for the new dimension of love and victory that the risen Jesus brings to all things.

The test of our presence with the living Jesus is whether we allow his presence to sustain us in all things. When we so live, Jesus' presence consecrates — that is, changes — our lives: his presence makes our lives something new, something they could never be by themselves. Human beings consecrate nothing in the eucharist; only Jesus does. We can no more consecrate our-selves to Jesus' service than we can make him our Savior and Redeemer, but we can accept his mothering of us and let him keep us. It is in the safety of that keeping that we experience Christian joy.

We must act in our lives, but it is not by our effort that we act; when we accept Jesus' presence in our lives, it is the activity of his life that animates us. In many restaurants, when the waiter or waitress places the entrée before the diner, he or she often says, "Enjoy!" If we eat the true food of the eucharist, Jesus' life in the world, joy will permeate our lives in the world. Joy will be shown in the world, but it will not come from the world, for it is a joy deep within us arising from the basic disposition with which we enter and meet the world. The joy arises from our life with Jesus, who has accepted us with a love deeper than our being or the being of the world. Christian joy has entered the world through an event that adds something new to all other events. Although the joy is available in the world, it cannot be destroyed by the world, for it is the excess of God's life over the world present in the world. It is called "love," and its effect is "joy."

If we were asked to name the most difficult thing to find in the world, joy would be a good answer to the question. Is anything more difficult to find in the world than joy? What more than joy in our lives would show that, while we live in the world, we do not live from the world? Christian joy arises from a source beyond us that overflows us. It is the mark of activity that refreshes us rather than tires us, and for that reason it is activity in which we can be said to rest. Joy is also something in which we rest because it is an end in itself; it does not exist to be used for anything beyond itself. Joy is the glow of love's presence; it is the present that love gives to the beloved simply because of love's presence. Joy is a gift, completely different from anything we can deliberately achieve or acquire. The joy that arises in our lives when Jesus' life becomes our life is the unique gift that Christians bring to the world, a gift that the world knows did not come from itself.

The immediate world of our fleshly lives is the world in which we are always making decisions; it is the world in which we are always doing one thing or another. It is into this world that God decides to come in Jesus, so that, in the Spirit and presence of Jesus, we can live within God's decision in our decisions. If we live in the spirit of Jesus, his Spirit becomes our spirit, and God's will then becomes our will. Then the risen Jesus becomes, as Paul said, a life-giving spirit for us (1 Cor. 15:45). When we live in Christ, the depth of God's life found in Jesus is given to our lives.

The breaking of bread and the pouring of wine in the eucharist are the ritual action of Jesus' life evoking the same action in our lives, if we eat and drink the right things — the true flesh and blood of Jesus — the fleshly life of Jesus in the world.

Sent from God, Jesus always acknowledged the reception of his life from the Father. To express thanksgiving for the Father's love and to show his complete dependence upon the Father, Jesus consistently said that he came to do the Father's will. Consumed by his love of the Father and his desire to do the Father's will, Jesus showed in his life a forgetfulness of himself in his relations with others. So present is the Father and the Father's will in him that the positive presence of God's Spirit in his life amounted to Jesus' death to himself. So completely living to God that his life amounted to a death to himself, Jesus was free to go to others and give himself for them.

All of those dimensions of Jesus' life in the world are found in the fourfold eucharistic action, in which Jesus takes bread and wine given by God, blesses them by giving thanks for them, breaks the bread and pours the wine, and gives them to others. "While they were eating, he took a loaf of bread, and after blessing it he broke it, gave it to them, and said, 'Take; this is my body.' Then he took a cup, and after giving thanks he gave it to them, and all of them drank from it. He said to them, 'This is my blood of the covenant, which is poured out for many'" (Mark 14:22-24; cf. Luke 22:19-20; 1 Cor. 11:23ff.).

The *taking* of what is received from God, *blessing* it by giving thanks for it, *breaking* (pouring) what has been so consecrated that it does not need to be saved for itself, and then *giving* the consecrated bread and wine to others constitute the eucharistic action. The ritual action freely willed and instituted by Jesus in his supper with his disciples is the very action of Jesus' freely willed life in the world.

Our participating in the action of Jesus' life in the eucharist is the way the *action* of Jesus' life enters the action of our lives. When we participate in the eucharist, we are taken into the action of Jesus' life already going on; our only responsibility is to remain in the action of his life once we have entered it. Not blocking the activity into which we are incorporated by letting it terminate in us is the way, as John's Gospel puts it, we abide in Christ. In the whole process, nothing originates in us or comes from us; our only responsibility is not to obstruct what Jesus does and to let the action of his life carry the action of our lives. His life in the flesh carries our life in the flesh when his decision carries our decisions. Having the decisions of our lives carried by the decision of God in Jesus' life is another activity — like joy — in which we can rest. Such rest is the peace Jesus promised to his disciples, a gift not given as the world gives (John 14:27); it is the peace of God that passes all understanding (Phil. 4:7).

The only question that remains to be asked is how far the metaphor of our being carried in the fleshly life of Jesus can be carried in our lives. To answer the question, we may ask another question: "Is anything more 'fleshly' than motherhood?" The relationship of an infant to its mother is an immediate, tactile relationship — flesh to flesh — of feeling, touching, warming, nourishing, sucking, hugging, kissing, protecting, holding, stroking, patting. Mother and child know each other in the flesh; in fact, in certain studies of mother-child bonding, 80 percent of the mothers were able, less than two weeks after the birth of their children, to identify their infants by touching the backs of their hands. Without the benefit of such a study, but with full knowledge of the fleshly intimacy of mother and child and of Jesus' intimacy with those who live with him in his Spirit, Julian of Norwich, as was not uncommon in her day, referred to Christ — especially in his merciful acceptance of us — as our mother. In her writings, Julian sometimes refers to God the Trinity as our mother, but at the moment our concern is with Jesus. Although Julian describes Jesus' death and passion as birth pains suffered for us, she also maintains that, from another point of view, Christians never leave the womb of Jesus. In this vein, she understands that "our Saviour is our true Mother, in whom we are endlessly borne; and we shall never come out of him."[1]

1. *The Revelations of Divine Love of Julian of Norwich,* trans. James Walsh, S.J. (New York: Harper & Brothers, 1961), chap. 57, p. 157.

[112]

In the process of physical birth we leave our natural mothers, but Julian says that, once we live in Christ, we never leave him; we are always kept safely in his womb. If we believe in the resurrection of Jesus, living his life in the world is the only true security we can know in our lives in the world.

The action of Jesus' life shared with us in the action of the eucharist is the womb of our lives in God's eternity. Because the womb of Jesus is a womb of grace, not nature, life in its safety releases and frees us in the world instead of keeping us from the world. Never to leave the womb of God's love for us in Christ is the ultimate security of our lives in the world. Living in Christ, we never leave our womb, but living in Christ means that we never have to protect ourselves from anything that may happen to us in the world. Thus, in the womb of Jesus, we live God's freedom in our lives in the world — able to be with others and able to go to others in God's love without fear for ourselves.

9

Jesus' Real Presence

WHEN JESUS celebrated the Last Supper with his disciples, it was not the case that Jesus was living his life and suddenly stopped in the midst of it to do something different. That is evidently what a number of people feel they do, however, when they go to the eucharist. Although the eucharist is most spontaneously thought of as a church service, it is actually the living of a life. The eucharist is not something we go to; it is something we live. It is not just a ritual; it is a commitment. The action of Jesus at the Last Supper was one with the whole action of his life — the giving of himself in thanksgiving to the Father.

In the Supper, the same giving of himself to others that constituted Jesus' whole life was made available to those to whom he gave himself in a new way. In his action at the Supper, Jesus made clear and laid bare the nature of his life in a new manner. During his lifetime, Jesus was misunderstood not only by his enemies but also by his disciples. In the Gospel of Mark, Jesus' disciples were almost always the last ones to understand what Jesus was saying and doing. At the Supper, in a manner that Jesus expressly willed so that his purpose could not be misunderstood, Jesus gave himself to others as clearly as he did on the cross. Jesus' will was the same at the Supper as it was on the cross, which is why, at the eucharist, we proclaim the Lord's death until he comes. The supreme gift of the eucharist — something not found in the cross — is that the glorified, risen Lord does come to us again! He who was dead, lives.

The Lord's Supper is now a ritual of the church, but its meaning is Jesus' daily life, not our representation of that life. Although a human being presides at the eucharist and says the consecrating prayer of thanksgiving, it is Jesus, by the action of his Spirit, who actually consecrates the sacramental bread and wine. Jesus' life is the meaning of the ritual: movement goes from the action of Jesus' life to the ritual, not from the ritual to Jesus' life. The impotence of many who want to live as Christians in the world today may be traced to their misunderstanding of the eucharist as a symbol of Jesus' life — a symbol they believe it is their responsibility to actualize in their lives.

The eucharist is not a shadow banquet; it is not just a meal copying an earlier meal. If the eucharist were no more than a meal imitating a previous meal, we could go to the eucharist and never meet Jesus; we would only hear words about him. But is that not what often happens? When we attend the eucharist, we go to a service and, at best, our primary attention is given to the book we are using, to the words on a page, or to the people who are taking part in the service with their varying degrees of ability. Such an experience is similar to driving in the rain and watching the windshield wipers of the car instead of the road ahead.

Driving is an action, and so is the eucharist. When we look at the windshield wipers while driving during a rainstorm, we know there is something — the road — beyond them, but it is vague, something we can only dimly see. We know that there is more out there than the wipers, but it is neither clear nor focused. The case is not dissimilar with the eucharist. We know there is more than the book and the words and the people taking part in the service, but we do not have it in focus — it is a blurred beyond. Such blurred eucharistic participation contributes nothing definite to our lives; thus it makes no specific difference in the way we live.

I do not want to press the analogy of Jesus' unfocused presence in the eucharist to the unfocused presence of the road ahead on a rainy night. But Jesus does call himself the Way, and, remembering that, we should focus on the action of his life in the eucharist rather than the words. Properly used, windshield wipers are a means of seeing the road; similarly, the words used in the eucharist are only a means to enable us to focus on Jesus, the Way.

Meeting and being with Jesus is the purpose of the eucharist, and that purpose should be our intention in our eucharistic participation. What should be the case, however, is not always the case. In sacramental theology, "proper intention" is said to be one of the necessary components of a valid, efficacious sacrament. All of the handbooks say that the minimal basic intention of the officiating priest at the eucharist is to intend what the church intends. Such a minimal requirement developed in sacramental theology as the guarantee to the faithful that, no matter what the subjective and personal views of an officiant might be, if he or she intends what the church intends, God's promise to his people in the sacrament will be fulfilled. The purpose of such sacramental casuistry is a good one: it is a way to guarantee objectively that the church is the ark of salvation, and that those who commit themselves to the church in good faith objectively have access to God's grace, in spite of what might be the heretical belief of an officiating minister.

The difficulty is that, once we begin to consider things objectively, we begin to turn everything into objects. The eucharist — like all the sacraments — has an objective dimension, but if that dimension becomes our primary concern, the eucharist is turned into an object. The sacrament becomes no more than something the church does. The eucharist appears to be a service, a thing in itself, and the proper intention of the sacrament becomes equated with properly putting it on or producing it. All of the words and actions may be theologically beautiful and liturgically correct, but one begins to wonder if the sacrament is any longer the *Lord's* Supper. When seen as a thing in itself, a service becomes an end in itself. Thus a "means" becomes an "end"; when the service is put on well, the end or purpose of the service is achieved.

No one consciously starts out to reduce the eucharist to an objective thing-in-itself, and the description I have just given is not intended as a charge against anyone. I do believe, however, that the tendencies I have just described are temptations we all face — and into which we all occasionally fall. When we do recognize such temptations in ourselves, the way to defeat them is to remember that Jesus, not the church, is the one consecrating the elements; it is Jesus who comes to us to let us into the ongoing action of his life. Even though we set the times of eucharistic services, we contribute nothing but a voice and gestures to what is really going on. Whatever is significantly done in the service is done by God alone.

The real intention of the eucharist is to intend what Jesus intends — his life — not a stage direction. Otherwise we turn Jesus' life into a ceremonial handbook. For years people have been told to bring their intentions to the eucharist; one was not properly prepared for eucharistic worship if he or she did not have a special intention with which to approach the sacrament. Whenever we are in the presence of Jesus, we are always present with our needs and desires, and intercessions for the world and ourselves — the prayers of the people — are properly offered at the eucharist. But a tendency of the piety that stresses our intentions is to bring Jesus' presence within the totality of our needs rather

test

than to bring our needs into the totality of his presence. We should bring our needs to Christ; it is not quite the same thing to bring Christ to our needs.

We will Jesus' eucharist by living it. We come to the eucharist to be incorporated into the fullness of Jesus' life in the flesh — into the decisions of his life in the world at hand. Our intention in the eucharist is to intend what Jesus intends. In that intention, we are moved beyond our thought into receiving Jesus' life into our lives. As Jesus said, his food was to do the will of him who sent him; as our food, Jesus' will becomes our will. We do the Father's will in him to the extent that Jesus' presence in our lives overflows our lives into the world.

To intend Jesus' intention is to will his eucharist; that is, we accept Jesus' coming into our lives with thanksgiving. Jesus' presence with us in the eucharist is always a new act of his coming to us. His presence is not the mere remembrance of his having come in the past; it is not a vague awareness of an unspecified presence everywhere; and it is not an anticipation of an unknown future. In the eucharistic action, we know Jesus' presence in an action as it occurs; Jesus is present with us as we share his action. The real presence of Jesus in the eucharist is neither an idea nor a spoken word; it is the penetration of our act of living by the action of Jesus as we do something together. As we and Jesus will something together, we live together.

As I have just said, all the sacraments have an objective feature. Sacraments are outward and visible signs objectively located in the world, and through them God offers his grace to his people with a certainty independent of human, subjective variations. As Jesus' physical body objectively located his personal presence in Galilee, so, in the eucharist, the consecrated bread and wine physically locate his sacramental presence for us now. Just as people knew where to go to find Jesus and to be with him during his life on earth, so we today know where to go to be with Jesus in a manner he specifically willed for that purpose. God's Word to us always comes from beyond us; thus God's Word is always a call to us to move beyond where we are in our life with him. Accordingly, leaving our pews in church to go to receive the sacramental body and blood of Christ reveals a significant mark of our whole life with God. God is constantly calling us to him from beyond us, and our hearing his call should show in our bodily lives in the world.

To be a human being is to be located. Knowing where to find a person is the first requirement for being with that person. Once we know where to find someone, however, our presence with him or her is much more than a physical relationship. The personal presence of two people with each other is a deep, interior relation that cannot be described in physical terms. Persons are present to each other as persons when they are present to each other as living subjects. Friends and lovers freely choose each other, and in that choice each shares with the other the spontaneity and singularity of his or her deepest being. Truly personal presence is the continuing free choice one person makes of another person; the delight and gratification of the reciprocal relationship of friends arises from the continuing free action of their wills. Such continuing action, because it is free, is a gift each newly gives to the other at each moment of their life together. Friends are those who will the same thing.

The eucharistic presence of Jesus with his people in the world today is a continuation of the intimate presence of Jesus with his disciples throughout his life. The mutual intimacy of Jesus with his disciples in all the meals he had with them — culminating in the Upper Room — was no doubt compromised by the disciples during Jesus' life, for, while Jesus first lived among them, they did not yet realize the full extent of his love for them and of his ability to be with them. The disciples' awareness of the depth of Jesus' love for them and of the intimacy of his presence with them awaited, to a large extent, Jesus' gift of his Spirit to them after his death and resurrection. The two disciples on the way to Emmaus became aware of Jesus' presence when he broke the bread at the meal they were sharing; this illustrates the beginning of the new awareness that Jesus' disciples had of the full reality of his continuing presence with them in his glory.

Once believers discerned the real presence of the living Jesus in the eucharist, differing views about the nature of that presence began to develop as the centuries rolled on. As believers attempted to understand their faith as best they could, theological schools and theological controversies arose. In the early church, the holy eucharist was known as the holy mysteries, and the ultimately mysterious nature of Jesus' presence in the eucharist has, to the best of my knowledge, never been formally denied by anyone who believes in that presence. But formal denial is one thing, and effective denial is another.

As attempts were made to describe Jesus' presence in the eucharist, more and more objective analyses were made of the eucharist. The presence of Jesus as a living person was the treasure the church wanted to protect, but as the church pursued that desire, an emphasis on the protection surreptitiously began to replace in importance the thing being protected. I use "thing" advisedly in the last sentence, for, as controversy intensified about the real presence of Jesus in the eucharist, his presence became more a thing to describe than a life to live. Impersonal, objective philosophical terms were applied to Jesus' presence. Thus, in the theory of transubstantiation, for example, the real presence of Jesus in the consecrated elements was described as an essential, substantial change in the bread and wine that took place beneath the sensual, external features of taste, shape, and texture, which remained unchanged.

For centuries, the issue in theological circles most immediately attached to the "real presence of Jesus in the eucharist" was whether one believed that a substantial change occurred in the bread and wine during the consecration, or whether a new substance was added to the bread and wine, or whether Jesus' presence was a spiritual presence in the congregation that made no difference at all in the bread and wine.

In such theological debates as I am describing, the means of Jesus' presence replaced the end for which Jesus is present. Theological engineering replaced Christian living. Actually, Jesus' presence, like every true personal presence, is a pervasive presence that expresses itself in many different ways through many different means at the same time. A person's presence can speak through every dimension of a situation: *she* can be present to him through her voice, her gestures, her appearance, her letter, her keepsake, her house, her special clothing, her special perfume, a place they went together. Anything or any activity in which her will was freely expressed can be the means of her presence with him, for she is most herself in the expression of her will. So Jesus is present with us in the expression of his will, but, because Christians believe Jesus to be the incarnate presence of God's creative Word, a fullness and an immediacy of Jesus' presence can be found in the expression of his will that are not found in the acts of our wills. It was in such a creative act of will that Jesus instituted the eucharist.

Just as we are present with each other in different ways, Jesus' presence with us in the eucharist is found in different modes; it is not limited to but one mode in the consecrated elements. True, Jesus' presence is uniquely located in the consecrated bread and wine; but Jesus is also present with his people in the consecrating activity, in the reading and proclamation of Scripture, in the ordained ministers, and in the people themselves assembled in his name (Matt. 18:20).

I have said that our intention at the eucharist should be to intend what Jesus intends; we do that by willing what Jesus wills.

"Jesus, I will your eucharist" is a way we offer our thankful acceptance to Jesus of his gift of himself to us, for we can will *his* eucharist only as our response to the gift of himself to us. When we will Jesus' eucharist during the eucharist, everything and everyone involved in the action of the service is being used by Jesus as a means of his coming to and being with us. Then, instead of other people getting between God and us — putting us off (or putting God off for us) by who they are — we see and hear God saying something through them to us. God shows himself to us and says something new to us through the otherness of the other person. To hear what God is saying, we have to listen to Jesus, not the other person. It is only in such seeing and hearing that we fully discern the Lord's body (1 Cor. 12:27).

In the eucharistic action, we spend time with Jesus, doing something with him. When we do something together, we are living with him. His presence with us continues over time; it is not found in just one place in an isolated instant — in the consecrated elements at a moment of consecration.

We envy those described in John's First Letter who saw, heard, and touched the living Jesus. But if we are aware of what is actually going on in the eucharistic action, we too see, hear, and touch the living Jesus. Those who ate with Jesus during his life on earth did not sit at the table with him with their eyes closed; neither should we, in the name of piety, keep our eyes closed during the eucharist. Seeing what is going on during the eucharistic celebration is an important dimension of Jesus' real presence in the eucharist. Keeping our eyes open is a dimension of our spiritual participation in the eucharist; in so doing, we will see Jesus give himself to all those who gather at his table for no other reason than to be fed by him. We will see Jesus give himself to sinners and saints, to those we like and to those we do not like, as well as experience him committing himself to us by placing himself in our hands.

Catholic theology says that Jesus is really, but spiritually, present in the consecrated elements. Such presence is an "objective presence," but that does not make his presence an object. After the elements of bread and wine have been incorporated into the action of Jesus' will, through the Spirit's action in the consecrating prayer of thanksgiving, the consecrated elements, enfolded in the Spirit, uniquely locate Jesus' willing, living presence with us. The purpose of the eucharistic consecration cannot be reduced to the changing of one objective nature into another; it is to make the living Jesus present with his people. Human beings never have known — and never will know — Jesus' mysterious nature; they know only his life-giving presence. It is Jesus' presence that makes the difference in our lives, and it is his presence that must be our first and last concern.

If we could isolate the presence of Jesus in the consecrated elements, the eucharistic elements would do what the grave could not do; they would keep Jesus' presence from the world. Jesus comes to us in and through the elements but not as the elements. As I have indicated, the life of Jesus is a located life because it is a human life, but Jesus' presence is pervasive and ongoing because he is risen from the dead. He lives, and he continues to live, with us. In the eucharistic action, we live with Jesus, like a person with a person, using time together. As I have also previously said, our only responsibility in the action is not to stop the activity into which we have been incorporated by coming to and participating in the eucharist; we have nothing more to do than to keep willing what Jesus wills and to continue doing what we have been doing with Jesus during the service. We do not return to the world to honor a dead man who once lived; we re-enter the world to let the Christ who now lives extend his living in the world through us.

In the eucharist, the living Jesus comes to us to incorporate our fleshly lives into his life. His life in the flesh is the womb of our lives in the flesh, and in that womb — which we never leave — we are nourished in a new life of freedom, victory, glory, and security.

It is just that that life can be received and lived only in the world at hand. It is a life that can only be lived; it cannot be achieved. That is our thanksgiving! That is our eucharist.

10

How Radical Is Radical?
How Different Is Different?

GOD IS GOD because he is different from us; that is why, when we accept God's presence in our lives, we become different. Christians distinguish the New Covenant from the Old Covenant by the difference of the new from the old. Those who recognized Jesus to be the Messiah saw him as the fulfillment of long-held expectations, but, as we know, the risen Jesus fulfilled old expectations in a manner not foreseen. It is commonly said that Jesus fulfilled old expectations by shattering them. His life was new wine that could not be kept in old wineskins; his life was a sacrifice that turned the accepted meaning of sacrifice upside down. In Jesus, Christians believe God radically and newly reveals his life to the world and shares his life with the world.

The words "radical" and "different" and "new" are words we frequently use in making distinctions between things and perspectives. Something is said to be new or different when it stands beyond or exceeds something else with which it is being compared. At the very least, every person in the world is different from every other person because he or she stands in a different place; and each of us has a range of viewpoints because of the varying heights from which we view reality. What I want when

I first see a tray of chocolate eclairs is not what I want when, having viewed reality from a higher level, I consider my cholesterol count also.

It is important to recognize the differences between things; thus, for example, when we are shopping for a computer or a car, salespersons primarily stress the difference — and so the superiority — of their product over other products. What is new holds an immediate appeal for us because of its intriguing promise to be something better than what we already have. But even when we are stressing the difference between two things, if we are to judge how different one thing is from another, we must hold both of them, with their differences, within a single framework. It is only against a common background that differences between things can be judged. We judge different household cleaners by the common criteria of how well they remove dirt, how much effort is involved, and perhaps how much they cost; we assess the different heights of children by a common measure of feet or meters.

Because we make judgments about difference and newness in a context that allows us to compare items with each other, a certain relativity always accompanies such judgments. What we judge to be radical is also qualified by a certain relativity, for roots penetrate to different levels, and what is judged to be radical at one level is not thought to be so at another level. How radically different one thing is from another depends upon how deeply the roots of the difference go. The first optical telescope gave a radically new view of the stars and planets; the development of reflecting telescopes was a radical advance over simpler refracting telescopes; and radio telescopes have proved to be a radical advance beyond all optical instruments. Similarly, quantum mechanics was a radical advance over Newtonian physics, and unified field theory, when and if it is discovered, will be a radical advance over quantum mechanics. In such truly radical advances, more phenomena are included within and explained by the new theories than were by the old theories — but the old theories themselves must be included in the new theories as special cases of them. In radical scientific advances, nothing is lost as science evolves; instead, something new is gained, for the deeper we are able to penetrate into the nature of physical reality, the more of that reality we are able to understand and correlate.

Because, as we have seen, we need a context within which to recognize anything we call new, fulfilling, shattering, or different, it is appropriate to ask what context allows us to use such terms to describe Christian revelation. Christians claim that the revelation of God in Jesus Christ is radically new from God's revelation of himself through Moses and the prophets; obviously, then, the Christian claim is made in the same context as Israel's claim to be the special people God chose for himself among the nations of the world. But the communality of the Judeo-Christian tradition goes deeper than God's choice of a special people among the nations of the world in Abraham, to God's creation of the entire universe in the first place. Recognizing God as the creator of the universe with its millions of galaxies, among which, in a minor solar system, our planet and all of its inhabitants are found, we should ask how the God acknowledged by Christians relates to the majority of people in the world who are not Christians. The mighty God, Yahweh, the Lord God of Hosts, whose acts are described in the book of Exodus, is a warrior who leads his chosen people out of their captivity in Egypt to the Promised Land, and who along the way slays — and is asked to slay — anyone getting in his people's way. The Lord of Hosts, for all his love of his chosen people, is a vengeful God who is asked to dash Babylonian children against the rocks (Ps. 137:9). The question is, How cultic can Christians be about their God, the God claimed to be the only God there is, the God of all people? Does God love some people so much that he will kill the innocent children of other people for them?

Is the radical newness of God's revelation in Jesus Christ radically new only within the historic continuity of the Judeo-Christian tradition, or does it relate immediately in its newness to all the people of the world? Jesus says that he is the Way; there is no other Way than he is; that means he is the Way for all people. Such being the case, we must ask ourselves how Jesus relates to all people in himself by himself, by virtue of his being God's Word made flesh, and not just through his disciples' efforts at evangelization and mission in his name in the world. It is so that our joy may be complete that we are to proclaim the Good News of God in Jesus to the world (1 John 1:3-4), but, if we are occupied in pleasurable pursuits elsewhere, does that mean God in Jesus is not immediately related to the billions of people who are not known as Christians? When the Word was made flesh and the Spirit was poured out upon the world, all humankind was newly and immediately related to God in Jesus, not just the few people who were the first to realize what was going on.

The question is, How cultic can we be about the only God there is, the God of all creation? The radical newness claimed for Christianity is claimed within the singleness of the Judeo-Christian tradition; does this mean that the difference can be known and experienced only within that tradition? Can a faith that is expressed in cosmic terms and that accepts a God who is said to be the creator and the recreator of the world properly allow a cultic piety either to fulfill or to replace a world-oriented ethic? Although Christianity claims its difference from Judaism in the common perspective within which both faith communities developed, is that difference significant in the eyes of the world? The secular world sees the radical difference claimed between the two to be only a cultic difference. Can it be said that the astounding difference that Christianity claimed for itself has now retreated to theological exposition and individual piety only, instead of being rooted in, and making a real difference in, the world? As I write this, Roman Catholic and Serbian Orthodox believers kill each other, in the former Yugoslavia, with a satisfaction they evidently feel is not only allowed by but blessed by God. Muslims, too, are being ruthlessly attacked, driven from their homes, and killed by Bosnian Serb forces. At the very least, the churches have shown themselves incapable of ending the ongoing conflict by invoking the name of the God whom at least some of those fighting each other commonly acknowledge. Much of the most heinous and inhumane killing the world has ever known has been — and remains — justified in the name of a god.

If Jesus is the incarnate Word through whom *all things* were created, Christians must understand themselves and all other people and things in the world to be immediately related to him; differences among people will then be accounted for by their differing awareness of that relationship rather than by a differing relationship in itself. If Jesus truly is the enfleshed creative Word of God, his presence is already everywhere, and, if that is the case, why shouldn't we recognize his universal presence by the way we relate to him?

The questions I am now asking are so general that they may appear to be leading us away from the reality of Jesus' presence in the eucharist. This is not actually the case, although the form of the questions may give that impression. My concern is with the nature and effect of Jesus' presence wherever his presence is recognized. Our concern is whether or not we allow Jesus to be present for who he is when we acknowledge his presence, or whether, in his name, we actually try to keep him from being himself. Now that I have raised such a possibility, let us return to an explicit consideration of the eucharist.

It is my contention that the greatest betrayal of Jesus' real presence in the eucharist is to make that presence objective in the

[131]

sense of turning it into an object, thus restricting it and making it less than itself. We have seen that the temptation to such reduction arises from the church's intention to protect the gift of himself that Jesus committed to the church in the institution of the eucharist. In its worship and veneration of its Lord, the church did not want Jesus' eucharistic presence questioned or profaned.

Who would deny that the most intimate presence of Jesus with his people known in this world, Jesus' eucharistic presence, should not be profaned? The crucial issue is to determine what the profanation of that presence is and how it is achieved. The point I want to emphasize is that what is taken to be a profanation depends upon the nature of what is being protected. If one is protecting something objective — something with no initiative of its own — then the responsibility for its protection is solely that of the person entrusted with the task. That person's judgment in the matter is final, for that person alone is the protector of what has been committed to his or her keeping. In such a manner, the church has become the eucharistic keeper of its Lord.

From the earliest days of the church, without exception, eucharistic participation and communion have been restricted. Reasonably enough, it was held that before one could participate in the holy mysteries, one had to be initiated into the mysteries. A lengthy catechumenate, a period of instruction and moral testing, developed in the early centuries of the church, and only those who had been properly instructed and tested were allowed to be baptized and to remain in the worshiping assembly for the consecrating of the elements and the consequent communion. The Didache, believed to have been formulated around the turn of the first century of the Common Era, states that the reason only those who are baptized can receive the holy eucharist is that it is not right to give such sacred food to dogs.

Consider now the protection of Jesus' living presence in the eucharist. For all the objectivity of Jesus' presence in the eucharist, his presence itself is not an object. If Jesus is really present, he is present as a living subject sharing the continuing action of his will with us. Jesus' presence in the eucharist is his continual giving of himself to the world because of God's love of the world (John 3:16). If the vulnerability of Christ is what has been committed to the church, protecting Jesus' vulnerability from the world — that is, preventing Jesus from being himself — is the ultimate profanation of his presence in the eucharist. When we seek to protect Jesus in this way, the judgment of our will about how Jesus should be protected from offense overrides Jesus' will to be himself; our judgment is then substituted for God's love.

Jesus' real presence throughout his life was acceptive, vulnerable, and daring. If the Jesus of Nazareth who was killed on the cross, who was raised from the dead and who still lives, is the same Jesus of Nazareth who is present in the eucharist, he does not cease to be everything he was. If the Jesus who once lived still lives, how could he suddenly cease to be offensive to those who now think they know his Father's will for him better than Jesus did during his life on earth? Jesus constantly offended the religiously pure and righteous of his day by eating with sinners. Was he not really present with them while they ate? The eucharist does not take its significance just from the Last Supper in the Upper Room; it is a meal that gathers and fulfills the significance of all the meals Jesus ate with others during his life on earth. As I have said, when we eat Jesus' flesh, we eat his whole life in the world.

Jesus constantly accepts and absorbs insults from us through the way in which we treat each other; do we think we are any less offensive to him when we try to preserve him from offense in our church services — with a ritual or ceremonial purity — than when we offend him with our actions during the week?

In the pouring out of the Spirit upon all flesh, Jesus comes to and is found within all human beings; that is why what we do to others we do to Jesus (Matt. 25:31-45). Jesus comes to us and accepts us, even when we attempt to live without him. Living by ourselves for ourselves, we do not merely neglect Jesus; we directly oppose him in our wills as completely as we can. In doing that, are we doing anything less than killing the one who comes in the name of accepting Love? Does the fact that Christ once died mean that we do not continue to kill him today?

Only in Jesus' love for us, offered to us in the very act of our crucifying him, do we discover an acceptance of ourselves so complete that we cannot fear betrayal in the total abandoning of ourselves to him. Only in the acceptance of us shown in Jesus' continuing love for us while we crucify him can we be assured that our self-abandonment to him is actually our self-fulfillment.

In our acceptance of Jesus' love of us, a love we have seen to be even deeper than our being and deeper than our knowledge of ourselves, we become aware that our previous attempts at self-protection actually amounted to our self-defeat, for such "self-protection" is, in reality, the separation of ourselves from Life too creative to be exhausted or defeated. That Life is not itself by avoiding opposition or even apparent defeat in the world; that Life is itself by accepting the worst that can be done to it and then making the attack upon itself the occasion of a new good. God's love never ceases to give, create, bestow.

⚘   ⚘

Two things should not be tolerated in one's religion: triviality and inconsistency. A person's religion should be the most important thing in his or her life, and for that reason it should consistently be itself at all times and at all places in his or her life. Consistency is a proof of importance. What a person is most consistent about is what is most important to him or her; that being the case, the consistency of a person's actual behavior may show his or her religion to be something different than he or she claims it to be, but the unmasking of the pretension occurs precisely because of the unbreakable bond that exists between a person's true religion and the consistency of its observance. What we are said to do religiously is what we do most seriously and constantly.

If we grant that the highest religious value in our lives is not something trivial and that we should not be inconsistent in our regard for it, we may nevertheless find a way to observe it that apparently renders that value important and allows us to be consistent while easing life a bit at the same time. Such an accommodation is achieved by giving an absolute witness to a religious value, but doing so in a restricted place and time. We could do that by limiting our Christian witness to a church service, or, in the case of the eucharist, worshiping Jesus' presence only in the blessed sacrament. If we were primarily to worship Jesus' presence in the consecrated elements, the consistency of recognizing Jesus' presence — and even the absoluteness of the presence recognized — would actually be a trivializing of Jesus' presence. The tendency to be avoided in the worship I am describing is the tendency to locate and restrict Jesus' presence in a manner that reduces it to something less than itself. An analogous temptation in theology, to which I have already referred, would be to consider Jesus' real presence in the eucharist primarily in the objective terms of a change of substantial essences.

A different type of trivialization of Jesus' presence in the eucharist occurs when we acknowledge his presence there but make it of no consequence. We do this when we are casual in our participation in the eucharist and in our attitude toward it, treating it no differently than we would any other social or communal event in which we may take part. "Eucharistic hospitality" that has no more significance than inviting someone to eat with us who happens to be in our house (read "church") at mealtime is an example of such trivialization.

In my years of classroom teaching and in the years in which I have continued to teach in my pastoral ministry as a diocesan bishop, I have tried to witness to the historical continuity of the church through the ages. Because the Christian life is incorporation into an activity going on before we enter it, being aware of what has been going on before our incorporation into it is essential for our participation in *it*. Jesus has been sharing his life with his followers down through the ages, and, if Christianity is true, its truth must be discernible through the ages. No one can deny that the church has erred and made mistakes in the course of its life, the most notorious mistakes having been made by ordained leaders within the church who attempted to claim that their individual views were the views of the whole church, but through it all the daily lives of the faithful have witnessed to God's love of the world in Jesus.

If we consider the continuing witness of the church as a whole through the centuries, I believe its life, truth, and vigor arise from, and reside within, the existence of the church as a eucharistic community. In fact, I believe there is no better definition of the church than its being a eucharistic community — which means that the function, nature, and structure of the eucharist are the essential function, nature, and structure of the church. The relationship and interdependence of all the faithful in eucharistic celebration are meant to be the relationship and interdependence of all the members of the church among themselves. Christians are themselves only in their relations to each other in Christ. The church as a whole celebrates the eucharist; the clergy do not celebrate it on behalf of the faithful. And it is the faithful — including the clergy — who celebrate Christ's life in the world in their lives in the world. The prayer of consecration in the eucharist is the great prayer of thanksgiving, in which God's people express their thanks to God for the gifts of his creation and for all he has additionally given them in calling them to himself in Christ Jesus. When we make Jesus' thanksgiving to the Father, at his meal with his disciples, our thanksgiving, the bread and wine in their way and our lives in the world in their way are consecrated — taken into the action of the Spirit and changed. Seen as the fulfillment of God telling his people through Moses that they were to be "a kingdom of priests and a holy nation" (Exod. 19:6, RSV), Christians are said, in First Peter, to be "a royal priesthood, a holy nation, God's own people," who consecrate the world to God by their thankful lives in the world and by their thankful use of the world in the Spirit of Christ (2:9).

Understanding the church to be a eucharistic fellowship means understanding everything in the church within the context of the eucharist. The fully Christian life, then, is the eucharistic life, and the eucharistic faith is the fully Christian faith. Contrary to much popular belief, baptism should not be viewed as the most inclusive sacrament. Baptism, for example, is not the context of the eucharist; the eucharist is the context of baptism. The initiatory rites — baptism or baptism and confirmation as the rites evolved in Western history — are the means of entering the eucharistic community; baptismal faith becomes itself and is completed only in the eucharistic life. Baptism in itself tends toward something beyond itself and more inclusive than itself; baptism is not the primary Christian sacrament that relegates the eucharist to no more than a service that baptized people sometimes put on together. Marriage, ordination, baptism, and confirmation are all most properly themselves within the context of the eucharist; penance sets us free from the past so that we may embrace eucharistic joy totally; and unction, the healing of the sick, is but a special application in our lives of Jesus' gift of his whole life to us in the eucharist.

In the eucharistic presence, Jesus is present; *the action of the eucharist is the action of Jesus' life.* As long as there has been anything that could be called theology, there have been disputed theological questions; in what is commonly called the scholastic age, some topics were so highlighted in theological debate that they took on a status of their own as "Disputed Questions." The proper response to a question is an answer, not a debate, but just as important as an answer to a question is the importance of asking the right question. Questions, like everything else, take their meaning from the context within which they are posed, and what would be a legitimate question in one context is not a proper question in another. For example, it would be nonsense to ask a rabbi of Jesus' day about the difference between strong and weak nuclear forces, for there was no context in the physical science of the time within which the question could be meaningful.

In these pages, I have maintained that the proper context for asking specific questions about Jesus' presence in our lives is our awareness of his immediate presence with us as a living subject, in the free action of his will. While, as I have said, there are many modes of a person's presence in the world, a person's presence in itself is always the person in himself or herself. It may properly be said that one person is objectively present to another person, but we can never properly say that a person's presence is an object. Truly personal presence is the presence of two living subjects to each other in the depths of their being as subjects, even though they may first have met by accidentally bumping into each other as objects.

I have asked a number of questions throughout this chapter, and, as might be expected, I have asked all of them within the context of the nature and manner of Jesus' presence I have tried to describe. If we try never to discuss Jesus or deal with Jesus in less than a truly personal manner, that context will change many of the things we say about him — and change many of the things we say we are doing for him. In fact, if we recognize Jesus immediately present in our lives, we will not be able to do anything for him, because it is he who will be living in us and acting through us.

It must be asked whether worship of Jesus that in any way removes us from the loving action of his whole life by turning him into an *object* of worship is worship of the living Jesus. Worship of Jesus removed from the action of his life is actually a distraction from him rather than an intensified awareness of his presence.

Jesus is never present with us as a static object; he is always present with us living his life of love, doing what he does: loving us with the Father's love of him, so that we can love each other — and all creation — with the same love. Jesus is the love of God incarnate, and love cannot be separated from what is loved. Love is a movement, a going to others; it cannot be contemplated or adored as an object in itself isolated from its action.

God did not send his Son to us so that he (God) could be worshiped as an object in a new way in the old world. God's love became flesh to change the world, to re-create it, thereby making it God's kingdom. Jesus' first words, recorded in Mark's Gospel, were *repent, turn around, change the direction of your lives, for the reign of God has now come into the world* (1:14-15). That is the Good News. Jesus comes to change us and the world, not to be a sacred object we adoringly protect from the world.

Where Christianity as a religion is concerned, we may ask the questions of how radical is radical and how different is different, but the only significant answer to the questions can be found by asking them about Jesus himself. How radically different was Jesus? Today we see Jesus as a much more radically historical, culturally located person in his time and place than did many Christians in previous ages. Current biblical studies stress Jesus' life and perspective as a Jewish peasant in the world in which he lived; the common world in which Jesus lived with others is increasingly accepted as the context that made him like, rather than unlike, other people of his time. It is only when Jesus' life is first seen to be radically located in his day that the scandal of the difference his life brought to others can be seen.

Looking at Jesus' life as a whole — at the kind of things he did and said throughout his life — John Dominic Crossan contends that Jesus' view of the kingdom of God is "more terrifying than anything we have ever imagined."[1] Crossan, representative of a large community of biblical scholars on this particular point, bases his claim on an analysis of Jesus' eating habits during his ministry and on Jesus' radical acceptance of other people throughout his life. In the society of Jesus' day, the rules about eating together and being invited to a meal were a strict application of the general societal rules for personal association and socialization. Jesus scandalized the righteous of his day by eating and associating with certain people. Studying the societal structure in which Jesus lived from the historical evidence available to us and by the discipline of cross-cultural anthropology, Crossan arrives at the conclusion that when Jesus said "Blessed are the poor," he was referring not to peasants living on the land — the majority of the population at the time — but to the lowest ten percent of the population: beggars, laborers, and slaves. Crossan summarizes Jesus' view of the kingdom of God as "a community of radical or unbrokered equality in which individuals are in direct contact with one another and with God, unmediated by any established brokers or fixed location."[2] Again representing a common view held by biblical scholars who otherwise differ among themselves, Crossan writes, "Here is the heart of the original Jesus movement, a shared egalitarianism of spiritual (healing) and material (eating) resources."[3]

Jesus' parables, his habit of eating and associating with the socially marginalized, and his uncompromised acceptance of

1. Crossan, *Jesus: A Revolutionary Biography* (San Francisco: Harper San Francisco, 1994), p. 73.
2. Crossan, *Jesus: A Revolutionary Biography*, p. 101.
3. Crossan, *Jesus: A Revolutionary Biography*, p. 107.

others throughout his life establish the fact that we are in the presence of a person who radically questions us and our lives. The living presence of two persons to each other is a dynamic and mutual activity in which each person spontaneously responds to the free expression of the other. Our one-way interrogation of the historical, objective record of a person who once lived but is now dead will never be the means by which the living Jesus is with us today. The real presence of persons to each other is the presence of living subjects to each other, not the presence of an object to a subject or of an object to an object.

If Jesus' eucharistic presence is his real presence, it is his real presence as the living person he was and is. In his presence, can we protect him? Is his presence to us trivial? Can we say that his presence makes no difference to us? Once Jesus' presence is recognized, no one will enter it casually, but if we truly bear witness to his presence in his presence, can we prevent anyone else from entering it?

In the light of our discussion, we may ask whether the right or the wrong questions have often been asked about Jesus' real presence in the eucharist. Could it be said at best that, in the objectification of Jesus' presence in the eucharist, the right answer has been given to the wrong question? But even if we make such allowances, we must ask whether or not the right answer to the wrong question is not actually the wrong answer from the point of view of the living Jesus.

❧   ❧

I have kept the questions we are asking general in nature, but I believe their specific application to our lives cannot be missed. These questions are questions we should be asking ourselves in Jesus' presence, or, better, they are questions we should let the presence of the living Jesus directly ask us.

In the exercise of my ministry of oversight as a bishop of the church, I tried to witness to the faith and doctrine of my community of faith as best I could. For such theological reasons as I have sketched above, and because of my understanding of the movement of the Episcopal Church to admit baptized persons to the eucharist without requiring that they first be confirmed, I frequently found myself in the position of having to explain to Episcopalians, as well as to others, that the Episcopal Church was not an "open communion" church. I was deeply involved in the theological explanation of why baptism alone was sufficient to admit one to eucharistic communion, but the change in admission to communion was a change the Episcopal Church made in its name for the members of its eucharistic fellowship.

The change the Episcopal Church made in admission to eucharistic communion was a change in the ordering of its own life; it was not meant to be an ecumenical statement operative in interdenominational relations, because eucharistic faith is more inclusive and specific in its wholeness than is the baptismal faith held in common by a number of separated churches. The eucharist, as I have said, supplies the context for baptism rather than baptism supplying the context for the eucharist. The eucharistic life is the fullness of the Christian life, within which everything else, including baptism, is located. The church is a eucharistic fellowship.

When people belong to different churches (denominations) because, among other things, they have conflicting — and even contradictory — beliefs concerning the nature of the eucharist, it is difficult to see how they can celebrate their unity in Christ in the eucharist. So it is that the Roman Catholic Church and the Orthodox Churches, among others, maintain that unity in faith must precede eucharistic communion among baptized Christians. When people hold differing views of what they are doing, it is difficult to see how they can celebrate doing "it" together.

In discussions with those who misunderstood the synodical

decision of the Episcopal Church about admission to communion
— including many priests and bishops — I frequently remarked
that I could consent to eucharistic communion much more open
and radical than was being advocated by many who were known as
theological liberals. But in the openness I could accept, *everything*
would have to be seen in a wider, deeper context, re-evaluated and
consistently adhered to.

In these pages I have begun to sketch the new context within
which I believe radical changes in eucharistic participation would
be justified. The "newness" of the new context I have suggested
springs from the acknowledgment of the literal and actual presence
of the living Jesus with us when we acknowledge his real presence
in the eucharist. We need to avoid objectifiying Jesus' presence and
trying to protect it as an object; instead, we need to let the accepting
nature of Jesus' presence be itself and live through us. The meaning
and significance of our eucharistic practice would change, I believe,
when viewed within this changed perspective.

The new perspective I am suggesting is larger and more inclusive than the so often objectively oriented perspective it would
supersede, but it is also more rigorous and strict than any purely
objective discipline we have seen before. In fact, its rigor and
strictness increase in direct proportion to the increase in its breadth
and inclusiveness.

If the past history of human response to Jesus' presence in
our lives — and of his presence in my life — gives any indication,
it may well be supposed that, because there is no way personally
to attenuate the pervasive rigor of the view I have presented, a
way will be found to dismiss it as being too liberal or lax —
objectively! If that is the case, we, like those before us, will be
able to locate and restrict our absolute commitment to Jesus'
presence in the eucharist in a manner that will at once enable us
to proclaim total commitment to Jesus but still not have that
commitment challenge more of our lives than we can handle.